BREAK THROUGH

FROM THE
STREETS
TO
SUCCESS

OMAR SHARIF

BREAK THROUGH

FROM THE
STREETS
TO
SUCCESS

wren
&rook

First published in Great Britain in 2025 by Wren & Rook

ISBN: 978 1 5263 6723 5

1 3 5 7 9 10 8 6 4 2

Wren & Rook
An imprint of
Hachette Children's Group
Part of Hodder & Stoughton Limited
Carmelite House
50 Victoria Embankment
London EC4Y 0DZ

The authorised representative in the EEA is Hachette Ireland, 8 Castlecourt
Centre, Castleknock Road, Castleknock, Dublin 15, D15 XTP3, Ireland
(email: info@hbgi.ie).

An Hachette UK Company
www.hachette.co.uk
www.hachettechildrens.co.uk

Printed and bound in Great Britain by Clays Ltd, Elcograf S.p.A.

For those who have felt stuck, lost, or uncertain —
you're only one breakthrough away.
May this book help you find it.

CONTENTS

PREFACE

Hey, my name is Omar Sharif. You don't know much about me, but by the end of this book, you will know some personal stories about my life that most people don't . . .

and you will have learnt things that can really improve, and might even transform, your life.

How do I know? **It did for me and for many others.** In fact, I have been asked by businesses and schools to teach the very principles I am about to share with you in this book.

I went through some horrible experiences as a teenager. Growing up in London, **I dealt with a lot of things most teens experience — peer pressure, lack of self-belief, making bad decisions . . . We all go through it.** But this also led me to some very dark places, and by the age of fourteen, I was in a gang. That could have been the end of my story. But it wasn't. I turned my life around and found my path to success. I never let it define or stop me. Would you believe I went from being an ex-gang member, homeless and unemployable, to being invited to visit His Majesty King Charles III in his home and being presented with a national award for my work?

I remember asking myself:

WHAT IS A GUY LIKE ME FROM THE ENDS DOING SITTING WITH THE KING OF ENGLAND IN HIS MORNING ROOM AT CLARENCE HOUSE?

Everything just looked expensive, from the ceilings to the chairs and the numerous paintings on the walls with their fancy frames. I felt like I didn't deserve to be there. But I had to change my way of thinking. **The truth is, I was good enough and I did deserve to be there, and you deserve greatness too. We all do.**

Since winning a __PRIDE OF BRITAIN AWARD__ and being handed my trophy by the boxing heavyweight champion Anthony Joshua (surreal . . .!), I have been privileged enough to share my story and coach thousands of people through all kinds of challenging situations, helping them break through fears and limitations and achieve **SUCCESS**. I hope to do the same with this book.

Success is a word that can mean different things to different people. When you think of 'success', what comes to your mind? **A Mercedes G-wagon? Being a millionaire? Having a Gucci or Louis Vuitton bag? Not having to work? Flying first class?**

Most people focus on the **huge** wins. I'm all about focusing on the **'SMALL'** but more impactful successes – like getting good grades, scoring a goal, going a day without getting angry, improving your health, becoming more confident, being happier more often. OK, they might not seem as cool as the Mercedes.

But I've found that the
more you stack up those smaller
successes, the more chance you
have of achieving great things
in the long term.

Here's something else I know. **BREAKTHROUGH** comes before success. Not only in the dictionary, but in life too. What is a breakthrough, you might be wondering? A breakthrough is a moment in time when a significant shift occurs, with the power to change the future. We can create these defining moments that change the direction of our lives. It has happened for me, and with this book, I hope I can help it happen for you too.

SO WHERE DO WE START?

Well, first up, I need you to commit to finishing this book, and here's why:

I want you to use this book
for your self-development as
opposed to your shelf-development,
as the Goodreads abandonment rate
has shown that 38% of readers report
abandoning books that they start reading.
If you can do that, you're already doing
better than 38% of other people
out there! Easy!

Secondly, I want you to think about the things that are holding you back. Are you feeling a bit meh about school? Got stuff going on at home? Have something you really love doing but you're worried your friends think it's stupid? Is there something you are embarrassed about, or maybe you currently suck at something? Or is it something much bigger, messier and more complicated? **It can be anything, and I'm not here to judge.** Just think about whatever is standing in the way of you achieving what you want to achieve.

Over the years, many clever psychologists have explored what drives human behaviours. There is one guy called **ABRAHAM MASLOW**, who came up with the **hierarchy of human needs**, which is basically a pyramid that shows the things humans need in a certain order, like **food and safety**, then **love and confidence**, before they can fully **grow and reach their potential**.

There is also **TONY ROBBINS**, who came up with the idea of **six core human needs** that drive and shape us.

And if you go way back, the famous neurologist **SIGMUND FREUD** came up with the idea that **our actions and feelings are influenced by hidden desires and thoughts** in our mind, which he called the 'unconscious'. He believed that human needs are **driven by these unconscious desires**, especially the need for **pleasure and avoiding pain**.

All of these concepts have inspired my own framework. The way I imagine it is that we have these levers in our heads that control everything we do and the decisions we make, so we can fulfil fundamental human needs such as the need to develop, to feel love, to feel significance, to have variety, to feel safe and to contribute. To explore how to meet these needs, I've developed six areas that this book will focus on:

FOUNDATIONS (and how to build on them)

CONNECTION (and how to resist peer pressure)

RESPECT (with an emphasis on self-respect)

THE RUSH (why the right kind of uncertainty and adrenaline release is so important)

SECURITY (why real freedom and success starts with certainty and feeling safe)

CONTRIBUTION (why doing, giving and kindness are the keys to success)

Have you ever done something that you knew you shouldn't do, but you did it anyway? Have you ever been rude to someone who didn't deserve it and regretted it afterwards? Have you ever done something that you thought you would never

ever do, but did it and you may have even judged yourself for it? I certainly have, and I am guessing you have too. **WE ALL MAKE MISTAKES.**

What I've learned is that there are things within us that we can't see, needs that aren't being met, but they play a huge role in the thoughts we think and the actions we take.

Learning this was a **game changer** for me. Once I understood this, everything in my life started making sense:

THE GOOD THINGS, THE BAD THINGS AND THE THINGS THAT COULD HAVE BEEN.

I realised if I could develop good habits and opportunities, **I could feel fulfilled and create a future I could be proud of**. For me, being fulfilled means **feeling really happy and satisfied** because I'm doing what I love and what's important to me. I have since shared my framework with other young people, **and it's helped them feel safer, develop stronger relationships and find the right path to**

success. It's also helped others convince friends who they're worried about to make better decisions and to stand by their side.

THIS BOOK IS MY COMMITMENT TO HELPING YOU TOO. I will be sharing my own life experiences growing up in London and navigating all the challenges every teen goes through, a lot of which you will likely relate to. But I will also show you how I took the wrong path. A path where I thought carrying a knife offered me protection, belonging, family. That was until three of my friends were murdered and I nearly lost everything too.

I hope by sharing these stories and my framework, I can show you that we all make mistakes but it's never too late to turn things around. That we all need to **BELIEVE IN OURSELVES** and find **CONFIDENCE** in our abilities. And that no matter what you might be going through — whether it be the really bad stuff or just feeling a bit directionless and lost — **you can find your way.**

I often ask people:

WHO do you want to BE in the next five years?

If you looked at yourself five years from now, what would you like to be **PROUD** of? What problems would you have **OVERCOME**? What **SKILLS** would you have developed? What would you like others to say about **YOU**? What would be **DIFFERENT** about you?

I'M ASKING YOU THESE QUESTIONS BECAUSE I KNOW WHAT IT FEELS LIKE TO LIVE IN FEAR OF THE FUTURE. NOT KNOWING WHAT WILL HAPPEN TOMORROW, BEING SCARED I WOULD BE A FAILURE, NOT HAVING A PLAN.

The first place to start is by understanding who you want to **become,** and I realised this when I was seventeen years old, kind of by accident. One of the worst nights of my teenage years gave me a gift. Let me share with you how it all happened . . .

INTRODUCTION

It was 7 p.m. I had just snuck on to a bus through the back door because I couldn't afford the fare. **I was desperate.** All I wanted was to go home after what I had been through. I ran upstairs, sat at the back of the bus, pulled my New Era cap low over my eyebrows and **tried to hide the tears in my eyes**. I rested my head against the window, watching the raindrops gather and streak across the glass. I **felt sad, scared and nervous. ANXIOUS** that at any moment a bus conductor would come and check if I had a ticket.

Soon the bus started filling up and I could see the expression in people's eyes when they contemplated sitting next to me, or even near me. What made me **SAD** was that at that moment, **I could have really used some form of emotional support.**

The truth was, *I HAD JUST BEEN ROBBED AT KNIFE POINT. I HAD RUN FOR THIS BUS IN AN ESCAPE FOR MY LIFE BEFORE THINGS ESCALATED.*

But still, on the bus **people were scared of me. I hated the looks I was getting for doing nothing wrong.** I wasn't acting a fool; I was just a teenage kid wearing my fake black Nike tracksuit and Nike Rift trainers I'd got from Wembley Market. **I hated what had just happened to me and, worst of all, I hated that I had absolutely no idea what path I was going down in my life or what my future looked like.**

ONLY THREE WEEKS PREVIOUS, I HAD DECIDED TO STOP CARRYING A KNIFE AFTER WITNESSING SOMETHING SO TERRIBLE IT MADE ME PROMISE NEVER TO CARRY A WEAPON AGAIN.

Now I'd found myself in another situation where my life was at risk. They'd taken my iPod, my W600i phone and my Oyster card. They'd even taken the £3.20 I had in coins — enough to get me a Jamaican beef patty, a portion of chips drowned in burger sauce, a can of Rio and a packet of wine gums.

I'D NEARLY BEEN KILLED FOR £3.20.

I held on to the orange handle on the seat in front of me, seeing names, messages and pictures of body parts scratched into the plastic on the back of the seat. There were even burn marks from people holding lighters against the plastic. One bit of graffiti that stood out to me was:

'*MAX WOZ ERE 2009.*'

I'm sure he meant 'Max was here'. But that message really got me thinking. Thirty minutes prior, someone had been **holding a knife towards me, making me empty my pockets in front of his group of friends.** Why had this happened to me? Well, apparently, being alone in a different area was good enough reason to get moved to – I believe people call it being **'G-checked'** now.

What if I had been stabbed? Who would have found me first? How long would it take until my parents found out? But also, what would people say about me?

What if **'OMAR WOZ ERE'** was written on my headstone? **What would I have achieved with my life?**

I sat there fuelled with anger. But for the first time, something in me switched as I really asked myself what **I wanted to achieve with my life and who I had to become**. That question gave me a sense of focus as I projected into my FUTURE, **looking at the person I wanted to be**. I didn't have a clear idea of who that person was, **BUT I HAD A VERY GOOD IDEA OF WHO I DIDN'T WANT TO BE, AND THAT FELT LIKE A GOOD PLACE TO START.**

As the bus pulled up to my stop, I rang the bell and made my way to the door downstairs. As I approached, **a woman clutched her handbag tightly**, forcing it under her elbow, probably fearing that I would steal it. **THIS HURT ME.** But I looked at her and said, '*I hope you have a lovely evening.*' Instantly, she stopped clutching her bag, her arm loosened and I caught the **glimpse of a smile**. I wondered if I had changed her perception of me.

WHEN I SAY 'ME', I'M TALKING ABOUT THE STEREOTYPE I REPRESENTED OF BEING A YOUNG BLACK TEENAGER.

It was still raining heavily, so I stood underneath the bus stop for a while trying to shake off the stress, and as I did, I saw myself in the reflection of the half-broken billboard, flickering every four seconds. I looked at myself, and I mean really looked at myself, and it was in this moment that I decided to break the stereotype of what it meant to be a young Black boy growing up in the city of London. Not to say that only we have it hard, but the struggle was real.

I KEPT LOOKING AT MY REFLECTION, ASKING MYSELF IF I WAS GOOD ENOUGH TO HAVE A BETTER LIFE OR IF I WAS CURSED. MOST OF ALL, I WAS ASKING MYSELF IF COULD I ACTUALLY DO IT — COULD I CHANGE, COULD I BECOME SOMEONE I WOULD BE PROUD OF?

In that moment, the broken billboard with the flickering light switched from a Subway advert to a Nike advert and those were the only three words I needed to read: *JUST DO IT*.

I convinced myself that I would be on TV, in the newspapers, and that it wouldn't be because I had been stabbed or had stabbed someone, but because I'd done something amazing with my life. I decided I would become successful and live a fulfilled life.

I had no idea what that would be or where I would start. **But fourteen years later, as I sit writing this introduction in an overcrowded coffee shop in Warsaw, Poland,** I can see myself reflected in the glass panels beside me. It's also raining heavily, and I am imagining myself back at that bus stop, looking at my reflection.

But this time, seventeen-year-old Omar can see grown-up Omar in his reflection. He's a little taller, has more facial hair, finally developed some decent enough pectoral muscles. We both smile at each other and say in unison:

'WE DID IT.'

I realise that I am now the person I couldn't see back then, and **I am very different to the person I was**. I am still myself, but there were certain things I wanted to change, and it seems that I figured out how to do it. I am now imagining seventeen-year-old Omar sitting opposite me in this coffee shop, and he is asking me if I have done what I convinced myself I would do. **I tell him that we have appeared on every major UK news channel, been published in newspapers, been invited on to chart-topping podcasts, won multiple awards** and been featured by online media platforms with over **five million views.**

I tell him that even though we didn't finish college or go to university, places like **Oxford University** reached out because they wanted to publish some of our story and our work in one of their national textbooks. I tell him that our journey and story has got us into some exciting rooms with amazing people who wanted to learn how we were **able to make the changes that we made**.

I tell him that there have also been **some really low times, and some extremely difficult situations** that we had to get through, but because of our decision to **constantly improve, to constantly grow, we got through them.**

Seeing young Omar happy in my imagination brings tears to my eyes, because all he ever wanted was to be accepted, to feel good enough, understood, and to feel like his life had meaning.

I also owe him **GRATITUDE**. The younger me was **BRAVE** enough to think **BIGGER**; he was **BRAVE** enough to not allow his surroundings to define him and limit his options. It was because he had such a **STRONG DESIRE TO LIVE**, to **BECOME GREAT**, that this adult version of me now exists. One thing that gave him this hope was his name — my name **— OMAR SHARIF.**

The name **Omar is of Arabic origin and means 'flourishing' or 'long-lived'. Sharif also has Arabic roots and means 'noble' or 'honourable'.** I was named by my family's spiritual teacher, Sheikh Nazim al Haqqani. I was curious about why he gave me this name, and so I did some research and realised I was named after the great **Omar al-Faruq, who was one of the most prominent companions of the Prophet Muhammad**. I bought books about him and studied everything I could get my hands on. **WHAT A MAN!** I thought, if I was going to do anything great with my life, then I needed to start by doing my name justice, and I set a challenge for myself. **The challenge was that one day people would know my name all over the world for me. (And not because of the Egyptian actor Omar Sharif.** You can look him up online . . . Even I am too young to know who he was!)

FUTURE PACING AND FINDING SELF-BELIEF

I didn't know it back then, but when I was seventeen and standing at that bus stop, I was doing something called **future pacing**.

Future pacing is when someone imagines themselves in the future in a desired situation. Not everyone thinks about or plans for their future. Some people just take things day by day and accept whatever comes. Other people worry about the future, forgetting that it hasn't happened yet and that the things they're worrying about may never happen. I needed to start consciously planning my future, and to feel excited and optimistic about it.

BECAUSE WHERE FOCUS GOES, ENERGY FLOWS.

I was still young and had the time to create something amazing in my life. There was no point in worrying about things that were too far off in the future, because I couldn't control that.

But I could control who I was tomorrow, and the day after, and in the coming weeks, until I'd steered my future in the right direction, becoming the person I hoped I could be.

To future pace, you have to **THINK REALLY HARD ABOUT WHO YOU WANT TO BE** and the specific results you want. For example:

WHAT WILL YOU BE PROUD OF? WHAT WILL YOUR GREATEST SKILLS BE? WHAT WILL BE DIFFERENT ABOUT YOUR LIFE? WHAT TYPE OF IMPACT WILL YOU HAVE? WHAT WILL BE DIFFERENT ABOUT HOW YOU FEEL?

This way, you can clearly paint the image of your **FUTURE SELF** and **get excited about becoming that person**. But you have to be real with it. It isn't going to work if your result is to grow an extra arm or to be able to shoot laser beams from your eyes. It isn't going to work if it's too far into the future either — **try thinking five years ahead, not twenty**. And it won't work if your result is too generic. Yes, we all want to earn lots of money, but it's not a helpful goal because there's not much to connect to on an emotional, intellectual, physical and even spiritual level. **Instead, go back to what success means to you.**

I saw myself already on TV, I saw myself winning awards, I saw myself speaking on stages and inspiring others. I saw myself not being in a gang anymore, not hustling on the streets. I saw myself being fit and strong. I saw myself being someone who people respected. I saw myself being financially free. And for each of those things, I could start seeing what habits I needed to change or adopt to get there.

The sad truth is that all of my future pacing was almost the opposite of my reality at the time. If yours seems like that too, then that's absolutely fine. Not being content with where you are can drive you towards achieving more.

The second thing you need to do to future pace is **visualise a different future for yourself**. When I was at the bus stop, I stepped into the shoes of future me and imagined what it would be like.

You can do this too. **Just imagine a day in the life of dream you.** Be that person and map out your entire day, from the moment you wake up until the moment you go back to bed. **Focus on the details, your emotions, what's new, what's different, who you might talk to, places you might go to. What's your confidence like? What are things that no longer bother you because you've developed a stronger mindset? How else have you developed?**

At some point every day, try going back to this visualisation, to feel like your future is already here, like it has already been achieved. The more you do this, the more you will connect with who your future self could be, and the more you'll see that it's possible. **Put your attention and intention on it, and make it happen.**

Finally, something has to shift within you to make a change. You have to **believe in yourself**. This is something that stands in the way of us all. We all have things we believe about ourselves that stop us from growing, from trying harder or taking risks that could improve our lives. We call these **limiting beliefs**. Do you recognise any of them?

I'm not good enough.

I don't fit in.

I can't change.

I'll never be successful.

I'm too different.

I have to be perfect.

People wouldn't like me if they really knew me.

I can't trust anyone.

I don't deserve happiness.

I'm not smart enough.

I can't handle failure.

My opinion doesn't matter.

I have to do it alone.

Everyone else is better than me.

It's too late for me to start.

I can't be myself.

I won't be loved if I fail.

I'm always going to feel this way.

There are more than a few in this list that I believed when I was growing up. As I got older, these became more specific too. **I believed I wasn't smart enough to go to university or to get a good job.** Where did this come from? For me, I thought it was a fact. No one close to me went to university or got a successful job, so because I was like them, neither would I. **I used other people's experiences to determine what I believed about myself.** Do you have any limiting beliefs? What are they based on?

Have a think about them and then reframe . . .

To do this, you need to really think about what the **TRUTH** is.

My reframe was: *THE TRUTH IS I am smart enough. I chose not to go to university because it wasn't for me, but I have skills and qualities that once people see, they will want to employ me.*

I would start saying this over, and over, **AND OVER AGAIN** until I believed it. Why? Because I had been repeating the limiting belief in my head for so many years that it became a pattern, and that's what we all do. **I needed to replace it with a much more empowering and encouraging truth.**

Here are the same limiting beliefs from earlier written as **empowering beliefs**:

I am good enough.

I belong and have a place in the world.

I have the power to change and grow.

I am capable of achieving success.

My uniqueness is my strength.

I am allowed to make mistakes and learn from them.

People will appreciate me for who I truly am.

I can find trustworthy people and build strong relationships.

I deserve happiness and fulfilment.

I am intelligent and capable.

I can learn from failure and use it to grow stronger.

It's OK to ask for help and support.

I have my own unique strengths and qualities.

It's never too late to start something new.

I can be true to myself.

I am loved and valued for who I am.

My feelings are temporary, and I can work through them.

I am a huge fan of putting things on the wall, so once you have identified and reframed some limiting beliefs into empowering beliefs, **write them out and get them on the wall.** Look at them daily, read them daily, believe them daily, because **they are your truth.**

Don't allow things around you to bring you down. **DON'T LET OTHER PEOPLE'S THOUGHTS, JUDGEMENTS OR OPINIONS STOP YOU.** Use them as energy to build your resilient mind. We are always going to have people in our lives who don't say the kindest things or don't show the best type of support, and some will just outright judge and hate on us. **But you can rise above it.** I remember how it felt trying to navigate my way through my teenage years, and I am glad I made it through them.

So that you can better understand why I do what I do now and why I even wrote this book, I'm going to rewind back to where it all began: my childhood.

CHAPTER 1

FOUNDATIONS - AND HOW TO BUILD ON THEM

As a child I didn't talk much. **I was very quiet and apprehensive.** My father used to tease me, saying that I was always standing between his legs, one hand gripping on to him, with a teardrop ready to be deployed at any moment. It's not that I was scared to talk; **I just remember being more interested in watching people – their interactions and their expressions**, and I absorbed much from this. Quietly observing and taking it all in but being a child of very few words myself.

But this led to another problem for me. Because I wasn't articulating my emotions through words, I felt those emotions a lot more intensely. Specifically, **MY ANGER**. This was a big struggle for me. Especially when I was arguing with my sisters, who were much better at communicating – **I couldn't match the creativity they had in cussing me, which left me frustrated.** What do you do with all those emotions when you can't express them properly?

I grew up with my three sisters, my brother and our parents in Central London. **I was always proud of saying that to people I'd just met, but the truth is, it only sounds posh.** You see, even in areas like where I grew up, which was basically a seven-minute drive from Buckingham Palace or ten-minute walk to Oxford Street, **there were two sides to it**.

THE SIDE WHERE THE RICH LIVED IN THEIR MANSION APARTMENTS AND, WELL, THEN THERE WAS THE REST OF US.

By 'the rest of us', **I mean those who lived in council flats**. Some kids at school got teased because they lived in a council flat, but I didn't see what was wrong with it. **All my friends lived in council flats, and it didn't bother any of us.** In fact, once they upgraded our building with a lift, it even felt like a high-end hotel. It didn't take long before people started destroying the lift, tagging their names in permanent markers and scratching the mirror with keys. But compared to some other flat blocks, mine was quite decent. It was a few storeys high, with brown brick balconies running across each floor.

It was relatively safe because each floor had some seriously heavy doors with dark grey grated bars on them. In some ways, it gave the building prison vibes, but it kept the wrong people out. At least most of the time.

We all knew each other. Some flats like mine would hang laundry on the balcony; some neighbours would leave their bikes in front of their doors. Some had nice plants by their doors; others even put deck chairs out when the weather was nice. **There wasn't much of a view, but I guess we made the most of what we had.** Sometimes, when the lift was broken, we had to run up the stairs, which was either good or bad. Good because the aroma of spices and slow-cooking food often filled the stairwell, making your mouth salivate as you sprinted up step by step. Bad because sometimes people also urinated on the stairs, so you would have to hold your breath and hop, skip and jump over those puddles!

But it was a proper community. People from all over the world lived in that block. Both my parents are Muslim – my father became a Muslim when he was quite young, and we were all raised with the teachings of Islam. My father is from two small Caribbean islands called Barbados and Grenada, and my mother is from Myanmar, which is next to Thailand. **It was always a little confusing when I thought about my heritage, whether I felt more Caribbean than Asian, or whether I was just mixed race but felt more British.** Whenever I had to fill out a doctor's or school form, there was no tick box that represented me, **so I had to select 'mixed other', which in some ways made me feel excluded.**

MY FATHER WAS MY HERO.
He was strong, athletic, extremely patient and an incredible salesman. At one point **I thought he was secretly Batman** because he had a 1973 Pontiac Trans Am, gloss black with a gold eagle on the hood, which all my school friends called the Batmobile! I was proud to have him as my father. Something he taught me was:

WHEN THINGS GO WRONG, DON'T GO WITH THEM.

He was always in a good mood, always smiling, positive — even when things weren't great.

And if my dad was Batman, my mum was Superwoman. She was a seamstress and set up her own business when she was sixteen years old. She juggled looking after us crazy kids with putting in hours of work sitting behind her machines sewing custom clothes, which have been worn by people all over the world, even royal family members. She instilled a sense of fear in us because we knew when we had pushed her too far, and we also knew when it was time to run out of the room before something flew across it in our direction! Old-school parenting. One thing she taught me was that **faith is the foundation of life.**

Both Mum and Dad had very little formal education, but they never used that as a **limiting belief** as to why they couldn't achieve something. **They were a team and they always had faith that better times were coming. This got us through the lows.** And the highs were really high — we were very lucky and went on some amazing holidays to far-flung places around the world. But then there were times when we really struggled. **At one point we were technically homeless, and we had to all live at my auntie's house.** She had a council flat too, and the seven of us all piled in to sleep on the floor of her small front room. To make it worse, someone had broken into my father's van and stolen thousands of pounds' worth of designer perfumes and cosmetics he planned to sell. **So we were homeless and broke. But they didn't sit around stressing the whole time – they put their heads together and made it work for the family.**

And it is one big family . . . I am the second youngest of five: my brother is the eldest, then there are two sisters, me and another sister. **We grew up close, but we were all different in our own ways and we were always competing with one another.** Competing to make my father laugh, competing to do the best homework, competing over who memorised more chapters in the Quran – everything! For a long time, I looked up to my brother. He was older than I was and always had cool stories about things he'd been doing with his friends, but I was too young to take part. **I often worried I wouldn't grow up to be strong like him.** My eldest sister was quiet but smart. She could read quickly and was a fast runner, always beating me in a race. My second eldest sister was a born entertainer. She lived in a happy bubble, making people laugh, singing and acting – and she was always in charge! Then there's my little sister, who was always affectionate and was a lot like me — wanting to be good enough for her older siblings and be accepted. **I felt protective of her.**

Finally, there was me. I never really knew what I was good at and **I had more insecurities than things I was proud of**. My bad eczema — a common condition that makes your skin itchy, dry and cracked — was central to my insecurity. My parents tried everything, from prescribed creams, private treatment, ointments and herbal medicine to holidays in hot countries so I could be in humid weather.

ONCE, ONE OF OUR NEIGHBOURS EVEN CONVINCED THEM THAT PUTTING CAR BRAKE FLUID ON MY SKIN WOULD COMPLETELY CLEAR IT UP. DO YOU THINK THEY TRIED IT ON ME? YES, THEY DID. IT MADE MY SKIN FEEL LIKE IT WAS BOILING FROM WITHIN!

The brake fluid got into the cracks on my skin and the only thing that helped was my mum running a bath of cold water, pouring pints of cold whole milk in there with bags of ice. I slowly eased into the bathtub and was so happy the pain was going that I didn't realise how cold the water was. **From this day, I connect cold to pleasure!**

But it wasn't just the eczema – I also had a stutter. It took me longer to start speaking than most kids, and when I finally did, the words weren't coming out in the same way they did when I heard other kids talk. **I would take a deep breath because I would try and blurt out everything I wanted to say as quickly as possible.** But I physically couldn't get certain words out of my mouth, especially words that began with the letters W or H.

WHEN I WAS IN A MOMENT OF STUTTER, MY HANDS WOULD GET SWEATY, MY EYELIDS WOULD FLUTTER AND I WOULD GET STRESSED. IT ALSO MADE MY ECZEMA WORSE BECAUSE WHEN I GOT STRESSED, IT IRRITATED MY SKIN AND THEN I WOULD SCRATCH.

I often wore my school jumper even in summer, just because I was embarrassed of the blood stains that would appear through my shirt from scratching too much.

PROVING MYSELF

There were lots of things going against me. I had the stutter, the eczema, and I was quiet. I wasn't the tallest in my year, I wasn't the smartest on paper and I wasn't the most handsome according to the girls. **But I wanted to be the best at something.** That something for me was athletics.

I saw how important being fit was to my dad. I couldn't even go running without getting a stitch or feeling sick, but I wanted to make him proud. My older brother enjoyed his food, wasn't very active and was overweight. **I knew deep down he wasn't happy, and I was worried the same would happen to me.**

With a clear aim of getting fitter and faster, I started doing push-ups, went for long runs, stole my dad's ankle weights and practised doing sprints. I noticed my training was going well when I beat my eldest sister in a race for the first time. I could now run around the block at a good pace and not panic or cry like I used to.

My father saw I was training and bought me a headband and two wristbands. **When I put them on, I felt like the man!** He wanted me to win the Sports Day race so badly that I no longer wanted it for myself — **I wanted to win so that my father could be happy. I wanted to make him proud.**

The day came. All the other Sports Day events had concluded and now it was the 60-metre race. I double-checked my laces were tied well, adjusted my headband and kept staring at the finish line, saying to myself: **I CAN DO THIS.** The whistle blew, and we were off. For the first 20 to 30 metres, the other fast guy in my class was ahead of me. I could see his knees reaching out further ahead of mine, but I noticed he straightened up too soon, whereas I stayed low and at an angle. **I KEPT MY FOCUS ON THE FINISH LINE . . . AND I CAME IN FIRST PLACE — A GREAT VICTORY!**

I was so happy, but I only really celebrated when I turned to look at my dad and I could see he was proud. I felt like the coolest kid at school in that moment. But the feeling of winning didn't last very long. I was constantly looking for the next thing I could excel in or that would excite me . . .

THE BAD GUYS

As I got older, I became more confident but often ended up doing the wrong things. **At home, I was a good boy. But in school, I thought I had to be cool and strong.** I had my first proper fist fight when I was in Year 6, I was excluded a couple of times for bad behaviour and **I could sometimes be a bad influence on others**. But I was also in the top set for most subjects.

In any class there was always a natural division between the kids who were focused only on their studies, the kids who didn't care about school and the ones who did care but started to become more concerned about what other people thought of them. This was who I became.

I started caring more about who fancied which girl, who had more muscle, who was the best at fighting . . . comparing myself to those around me and thinking about how I could be cool. I was still friends with the 'good guys' but began to be drawn to people I could be playful around.

By 'playful', I mean mischievous, cheeky or playing the class clown.

This soon spiralled – from sneaking into the local cinema and getting chucked out for throwing popcorn in the rows ahead to stealing sweets from the local corner shop. **It was scary, but it gave me a thrill and I liked being in a group** – all of us rolling together or even just plotting on the block.

Although I grew up in Central London, this doesn't mean it was safe. Yes, there were mansion apartments owned by celebrities and rich families whose kids went to private school, but there were also sprawling council estates and people who couldn't be trusted. As time went on, we started playing out in bigger groups and I could sense that **we were all competing with each other to see who was the 'hardest'.**

THE TRUTH WAS THAT I WASN'T HARD AT ALL. I HATED CONFLICT AND FIGHTING, AND I FELT GUILTY IF I HIT SOMEONE, BECAUSE WHAT IF I REALLY HURT THEM? I HAD SOME FRIENDS WHO WERE PRACTISING MARTIAL ARTS AND BOXING, BUT THE ONLY

EXPERIENCE I HAD WAS DEFENDING MYSELF FROM MY BROTHER.

My brother was different to me, and I spent a lot of my time **trying to be like him or good enough for him to acknowledge me**. I loved playing with our toys, and one day, me and my sisters were playing with my Action Man dolls and their Barbies, like a family. **For some reason this bothered my brother. He called me names, saying that boys don't play with Barbies.** This made me cry, but he said, 'Real men don't cry.' Because he was older than me, I trusted what he said. **And so I tried to hold in my tears whenever I felt like crying, or I would go downstairs, find a brick wall and start punching it.** I wouldn't stop punching it until my knuckles bled. And I did this for a long time. I started to embody the idea that crying meant I was weak, and all I kept thinking about was how could I be good enough for my older brother. **I was insecure and wanted to be accepted.**

But I also felt the pressure to be hard enough for the streets. People were starting to get robbed and beaten up in my area. There was a time when I was about eleven and **I watched my brother get into a fight**. I was standing with my back against a garage door, holding a bag of shopping from the market. He was to my right, and around eight to ten guys his age were on his left. They all started to circle him. **I felt scared for him and for myself.**

Out of nowhere, he jumped forward, grabbed the biggest guy with his left hand and put him into a headlock. With his right hand he started swinging and punching any of the other guys who tried approaching him, batting them all off. Punches were being thrown, people were dropping, bystanders were screaming for them to stop from the balconies above, and I was just standing there, frozen, taking it all in. **I felt totally useless.**

My brother let the guy out of the headlock and warned him that it would take more than ten of them to take him down. **Although I really disliked some things about my brother, at that moment, he had my full respect, because if I had been him, I would probably have calculated the odds and run.**

So now my question was, **HOW DO I BECOME LIKE HIM?** I didn't want to think or worry about fights and being safe. I really enjoyed playing with my toys and had a huge collection of WWF and WCW wrestlers. But all those wrestlers had strong, defined muscles. When I watched them on TV, the bigger the guy, the stronger he was. **So now I started thinking about how I could get bigger and what I could do to look like the toy wrestlers that I had.**

Whenever I had a fight with my siblings, I would run into the bedroom and stare in the mirror, fists clenched, breathing quick and shallow into my chest, **hoping I might transform into the Hulk**. I waited to see if my eyes would turn green, or if any muscles or veins would start bulging out, but of course this didn't happen, **and it only made me angrier**. I was normally naturally calm like Bruce Banner, but when I got angry, my emotions would completely switch, and I found it hard to control.

CHANNELLING MY ANGER

So if I couldn't become the Hulk or a wrestler, what could I do? **I started focusing on sport instead.** I continued jogging around the block and would often try to race my own shadow around the estate. I soon realised this wasn't going anywhere, so with some Eid money I had saved, I bought myself a vintage Casio digital watch from one of the local Saturday markets. **I could now time every lap that I did, every sprint and every time I climbed up the stairs to my flat.** Yes, I now chose to take the stairs. Proper Rocky Balboa moment!

I eventually started timing some of our family bike rides around Regent's Park too. I didn't really know how to get faster, I just kept doing what had worked for me before, **and each week I told myself that I wanted to beat the previous week's time** and would record my progress in an old blue exercise book from school.

There was no better feeling than seeing my time get smaller and smaller each month. I couldn't wait to get up at the weekend to go and time myself. And here's the thing - I was no longer as bothered about being 'hard' or 'muscly'. I wasn't doing this to impress anyone or to compete with people at school. It was something I started doing for me, and it became an addictive feeling because I felt strong and empowered.

It then got to the point where I was done challenging myself and I now wanted to challenge other people I knew to race me. Some of these guys were older than me and lived in other blocks nearby, but that didn't bother me anymore. **In fact, many things that used to bother me didn't worry me now.**

I still had eczema, but I learned to accept that it was only a skin condition; it was part of me. I had been called all sorts of names because of it, and I had previously imagined what it would be like to beat up all those bullies. **But now, I didn't feel the need to. I couldn't beat them up, but I could beat them in a race!** And instead of having conflict with me, they showed me some respect, which gave me a sense of pride. **When we set ourselves personal goals, our focus shifts, and all those challenges get that bit easier to manage.**

GROW THROUGH WHAT YOU GO THROUGH

I've been talking to you about my story, but I hope you can see ways it might apply to you too. Growing up, I became competitive, whether it was against my siblings or friends at school. I wanted to win, I wanted to achieve, I wanted to be better than them at something. I wanted to see that I could improve at something.

There is a reason for this. **All these things made me feel good, so I wanted to do more of them.** This is one of the core aspects that drive human behaviour — our need to develop and make progress. **It's crazy to think that you once didn't exist.** Your eyes, heart, brain, hands and feet were all developed when you were in your mother's belly. **Development is a part of life and it's crucial to our progress, because when we feel like we aren't growing or moving forward, well, life just seems to SUCK.**

I have mentored many young people who struggled with mental health problems and felt really down. All of them believed they had no skills or weren't good at something. **But investing your energy in getting better at something and making progress will NEVER make you feel down.** I don't care if it's building paper aeroplanes, counting how many kick-ups you can do, doing the moves correctly to a new TikTok dance, or running round the block and timing yourself like I did. **If you channel all your frustration into something positive**, you can try to improve and recognise that you are getting better and making progress. **You will start to feel happier.**

It's like playing your favourite video game. You start at level one, and it's pretty simple. **As you progress, the levels get harder, but you also get better at the game.** Eventually you get to a boss level, and you may get stuck on this level for a while, **but you keep at it,** and just like that you defeat the boss. The same thing happens in life. When you develop new skills or improve the ones you have, though you face challenges along the way, once you get there, **you feel a great sense of achievement, which makes you feel fulfilled and builds your confidence**. And when you develop new skills and knowledge, you open new opportunities for yourself. Again, it's like unlocking new levels in a game. **Each new skill can lead to exciting possibilities** — meeting new people, discovering new interests and even finding new career paths in the future. Development keeps life interesting and full of potential.

DOSAGE: Dopamine

When I share my ideas with schools, I like to align each of the core components of my framework with six neurotransmitters and hormones within the brain. These are:

DOPAMINE

OXYTOCIN

SEROTONIN

ADRENALINE

GLUTAMATE

ENDORPHINS

Or, as I like to call them, **DOSAGE** for short. **A neurotransmitter is a special messenger, or chemical, that carries important messages around your brain,** like a super-fast courier. Alongside lots of other factors, neurotransmitters impact human behaviour, making us act in certain ways — **sometimes good and sometimes bad**. The neurotransmitter I want to talk about here is **DOPAMINE**, which is one of the big drivers of your brain's reward system, and which you might have heard about in relation to social media and technology.

All those things I did, such as getting faster and winning the race, **made me feel good, and so I wanted to do more of them. This was driven by dopamine, which gives us feelings of pleasure, satisfaction and motivation.** Dopamine is triggered and starts getting released even when we think about something that gives us pleasure, which then motivates us to do that thing! It is also released while we're feeling pleasure and even afterwards.

We are all addicted to dopamine and receive it in our own ways. In life we don't just do things or want things for the thing itself. **We do them for the feeling we think those things are going to give us.** For example, my goal was to be the fastest boy in my school. **The excitement and motivation for that goal was also stimulated by dopamine.** The motivation I had during my training for that race was stimulated by the pleasure I knew I'd receive by winning the race. And then the excitement of celebrating after the race was reinforced by another huge release of dopamine.

SO, THE HABITS AROUND THE FAVOURITE FOODS YOU LIKE TO EAT, SHOWS YOU LIKE TO WATCH, GAMES YOU LIKE TO PLAY AND PEOPLE YOU LIKE TO BE AROUND ARE ALL INFLUENCED BY THE PRESENCE OF DOPAMINE IN YOUR BRAIN.

This can be a good thing, but it also means you can attach pleasure to things that are bad for your health, your safety and ultimately your life.

Think about your iPad or smartphone. The constant needing to know who has liked your most recent pic, commented back or followed you. The noise of that ping or the colour of the notification suggesting you have ten new likes **keeps feeding your dopamine addiction.** It feels good because you feel seen, your content is being liked by others so you're getting **external validation**, and your account is growing so you feel like you are becoming more important. **It's addictive. But it's also harmful – slowly impacting your self-confidence, your concentration and more.**

It's the same with being the class clown, being rude or being loud. **Some people love the attention they get from it** – I know I did – which makes them want to do it more. **But what happens later on?**

They might not get the required grades to get a good job, they might end up working a job that they don't like, or they might find they end up with few friends, because people actually just find them annoying. It's the same with people who want a fight - they get addicted to the feeling of power, respect and the rush of adrenaline (another neurotransmitter - more on that in chapter 4) that is released when they throw that punch. And it's the same for more harmful addictions to substances such as alcohol and drugs.

But it's possible to trigger these neurotransmitters in good ways and build positive habits that make you feel good and help you progress. For most of my childhood, I felt insecure and not good enough, and that fuelled me with a desire to grow, to develop, to change. **As you'll find out later in this book, there are plenty of times I made the wrong move and ended up in really bad situations** – doing things that made me feel good in the moment but were hugely damaging in the long term.

BUT LIFE IS ALL ABOUT DEVELOPMENT AND PROGRESS.

YOUR PERSONAL BEST

Feeling like you're developing is important because it keeps you working towards something and it maintains the idea that you're on a journey. **So if you find that you are constantly unhappy, start focusing on something that you can get better at and begin improving.** This could be your studies, a hobby, a relationship, a job, a skill or learning something new. For example, if you know that there's a sport that you like playing but you don't play it much because you're not that great at it **YET**, don't sit and think about how rubbish you are. **Instead, find times in the week to go and practise that sport until you get better.** Watch YouTube clips on how to boost your skills. **Once you start noticing that you're improving, watch what it does to your attitude and confidence.**

Remember, improvement is an ongoing competition with yourself, not with anybody else – that's why it's called **self-improvement**. Not everyone has the capability to win Sports Day, be top of the class or dazzle in drama, music or dance, but every single one of us is capable of being better than we were yesterday, of putting in the work to ensure we're that little bit better tomorrow.

Athletes are constantly striving to achieve **personal bests**, but a personal best isn't some special achievement available only to top sports stars. **It is simply about doing the best you've ever done at anything so far.** Whenever I was timing my runs on my new Casio watch or recording my bike rides around Regent's Park in my exercise book, I was clocking faster and faster times, which were all new personal bests for me. **They're the measure by which I can see I'm improving, and they give me that dopamine hit my mind craves as a reward.** Personal bests can just as easily be measured by improving grades, getting more positive feedback from a teacher or parent or coach, swimming five or ten metres further then you could last week or getting that little bit closer to nailing a dance or gymnastic move you haven't yet mastered. **They're all measures that show you're improving!**

Do it for long enough and you might find you have one of those **BREAKTHROUGH** moments I talked about at the beginning of this book, when you've improved so much that your landscape changes completely **and you change the course of your own future**. You realise how much better you feel, how dedicated you are to improving this aspect of your life, **and it becomes a huge source of happiness.**

If you want to keep feeling happy, then keep finding things to get better at – it's really as simple as that. Peer pressure from friends can very easily lead you to make poor decisions purely because if you do that thing, then you feel you've got the validation of others. **I was the same when I wanted to be more like my brother.** But think about what habits or hobbies you can start doing for you, **NO ONE ELSE.** Just like how I shifted my focus on to getting fitter, faster and winning races, not for the external validation of others, but because it instilled me with my own sense of self-belief. **This made me realise I was good enough.**

I wasn't lucky to get to where I am now; I just never stopped. There were many moments when I felt like giving up, and as you continue reading this book, you'll understand why. But there was always something in me that believed that lacking passion comes from playing it safe and settling for a life beneath your potential rather than embracing the full extent of what you can achieve. **You can start this by creating new habits that will help you on your path to progress.**

CHAPTER 2

THE NEED TO BELONG AND CONNECT - AND THE COST OF GETTING IT WRONG

I was in Year 9, and it was wood tech design class. We were supposed to be building some sort of supportive frame, but all I could think about was what was happening after school. Instead of sanding down wood and gluing sticks together, my friends and I waited till the teacher wasn't looking and slowly slipped whatever heavy and sharp pieces of equipment we could find into our bags. I had two files up each of my blazer sleeves, a sharp picking device and a type of clamp. You might be wondering, were we taking these things so that we could work on our projects after school?

Unfortunately not. There was a different type of project going on: one that could end in people getting very hurt.

That was just first period. I was tense the whole day. My eyes were glued to the clock, and I was thinking about what was going to happen later. **As I walked around during break and lunchtime, I could see people gossiping about it too.**

Even though we were in one secondary school, there were still **pockets of division, normally split by race**. In my school we had the Black kids, the Kurdish kids and the Bangladeshi kids. **It's not that we were at war with each other, but people tended to stick with people who were like them.** I didn't like to create division — I was cool with everyone, mostly because, yes, I am Black, so naturally I connected with the Black kids, but my faith created a bond between myself and the Kurdish and Bangladeshi kids. **By Year 9 I'd almost accidentally built a reputation for myself and I had some respect.**

This hadn't always been the case. In Year 7, I had no street rep. I was shy, quiet and really only stuck with my main circle of friends. In Year 8, I started to develop more confidence but still felt that I was too soft, and I wanted to be known as a cool guy who got attention. By Year 9, things had changed . . .

It was lunchtime and I had three hours to round up as many guys as possible. I already knew my Black brothers would have my back. I went to speak to my Kurdish and Bangladeshi brothers to ask them for the same thing.

And when I say 'have MY back' — that's exactly what I mean, because I was central to what was happening.

Let me break down what was going to happen. Because of this reputation that I had built for myself, and because of a confrontation that had happened two years before, there was a question going around about who would win in a fight between me and another 'HARD' guy from a different school. When people asked me who I thought would win, of course my response was me, but inside I wasn't sure at all. **I still hated fighting and confrontation deep down, but I felt like I had to appear as if I had no fear.**

We heard that there were at least two buses full of students from the other school coming. So, I told everyone to make sure they were tooled up, meaning that **everyone carried weapons**. One of my Kurdish friends showed me that during second break, one of his cousins had slipped in a **bag full of blades through the gate in the playground**, as his uncle owned a barber shop. This curiosity about who was the 'HARDEST' was turning into a war, **a war that could cost someone's life**.

The truth is, I had no curiosity about who would win. I didn't care, this guy wasn't from my area, our lives never had to cross. **I had agreed to this because I felt the peer pressure to rep my school.**

It was 3 p.m. We were all sat in our tutor group classes. My eyes were fixed on the small hand of the clock ticking away. **I was nervous.** My knees were bouncing underneath my desk; my brain was racing. And then something else hit me. I thought:

IF SOMETHING DOES HAPPEN TO ONE OF US OR THEM, OUR PARENTS ARE AT HOME RIGHT NOW AND WILL WONDER WHERE WE WERE, ONLY TO HAVE US NEVER RETURN.

I imagined my mum waiting for me and getting worried, not knowing where I was or what had happened. **But those thoughts only made me more fearful, and now wasn't the time for fear.** I had to focus on things that put me in the right state of mind. I looked at my boys in class, and they put their right fists to their chests, signalling to me that they'd got me. **I took comfort in that.**

The school bell rang. It was time. I left my tutor group room, **not knowing if I would return**, but again the thought of me winning took over. I would have the ultimate reputation and **I was hungry for that**. I wanted to show my brother that his lil bro had road rep now. I got outside the school gates, and nobody was going home — **everybody wanted to come and see what was going on.**

Not a lot of words were exchanged. **WE LOOKED INTO EACH OTHER'S EYES, NODDED OUR HEADS IN ACKNOWLEDGEMENT THAT IT WAS TIME.** We were going to meet at the top of Church Street Market, which was a five-minute walk away.

We made our way there. We got the text message that the **two buses full** of students were on the way and more were waiting for the next bus. We had more guys ready to jump in from a block of flats near Church Street, who were told to stay out of sight for now and to only come out once the other school were all there, as we wanted to attack them from the back. **Like I said, this was becoming a war.**

We were walking through roads, making cars stop. Anybody who was on the same side of the pavement crossed over to the other side. **It was a powerful and addictive feeling, to know we had such a presence.** I walked with several guys who were also considered the hardest in the school. They were trying to plan who was going to do what and who was going to take on who.

We got to our meet-up point. The kids from the other school weren't there yet, so I started mulling things over in my head. Like, was this a set-up? Were they coming from somewhere else? Who else were they bringing? But then the buses arrived. **Kids poured out of them, almost as if the buses had three decks instead of two.** I was scanning as many faces as possible from across the street until I saw the other guy. **Then our eyes locked.**

Automatically, guys from my school started shouting the name of our school. **The guys from the other school were shouting the name of theirs, and we were insulting each other with swear words.** Me and the other guy got face to face, and things went quiet. **This was the moment everyone had been waiting for.** It went a bit like this . . .

ME: Y'KNOW YOU'RE NOT IN YOUR ENDS, YEH?

BOY: DATS CALM, FAM. WE'RE HERE, INNIT.

ME: CALM, SO WHAT YOU ON?

BOY: WHATEVA YOU'RE ON, INNIT.

ME: YOU CAME ALL DIS WAY, FAM. I'M HERE, SO WHAT YOU TELLIN' ME?

BOY: CERTAIN MAN SAID YOU COULD HAVE ME, SO HAVE ME DEN.

ME: CERTAIN MAN SAID YOU'D KNOCK ME OUT WITH ONE PUNCH. DO YOUR THING DEN.

At this point, I looked over his shoulder and I recognised one of the guys standing there. He was one of my friends from primary school; we used to play with our WWF toys together at his house. He had a bandana covering his face but I knew it was him, so I said to him:

ME: RAH, SO YOU'RE BACKING HIM NOW, YEH. I THOUGHT WE WAS BOYS.

BOY 2: BUN DAT. PRIMARY SCHOOL IS OVER, G.

ME: OK, COOL, YOU'RE A SNAKE, YEH. WATCH.

BOY: DIS IS BETWEEN US. MAKE YOUR MOVE.

ME: I'M STANDING RIGHT IN FRONT OF YOU. MAKE YOUR MOVE AND THEN WATCH WHAT HAPPENS.

BOY: HIT ME FIRST DEN.

ME: YOU HIT ME FIRST.

BOY: ARE YOU SHOOK OR WHAT?

ME: IS THAT WHY YOU'RE NOT HITTING ME, BECAUSE YOU'RE SHOOK?

BOY: DON'T EVER CALL MAN DAT.

ME: OR WHAT? STOP TALKING AND DO WHAT YOU CAME HERE TO DO.

People from both schools were cheering us on, saying, **'GO ON, JUST PUNCH HIM, START IT, START IT.'**

We stood there, chests puffed up, fists clenched, eyes locked. My heart was racing in anticipation.

BOY: PEOPLE CAME HERE TO SEE A TING.

ME: I'M NOT STARTING IT. MAKE YOUR MOVE AND THEY WILL SEE A TING.

BOY: I'LL SHOW YOU WHAT MAN'S ON IF YOU START IT.
ME: I DON'T HIT FIRST.
BOY: ME NEITHER.

The crowd was getting impatient because they wanted someone to throw the first punch. I had one hand behind my back, which was where I was keeping one of the tools ready just in case he had a weapon. **It was at this point that I felt someone behind me unclench my fist and slip a knife into my hand.**

Another person whispered in my ear, *'Come on, Omar man. They're in our bits, bruv. Slice him and then we will deal with the rest of them easy.'*

We were still standing face to face, about a foot apart. **I had never used a knife before and I knew I wasn't going to use it.** I tracked his movements carefully, seeing where he put his hands, watching to see if he would draw back to throw a punch, or if he would twist his body in preparation.

It got to the point where I knew he wasn't going to make the first move and neither was I, but someone from his school threw something, which landed on one of our guy's heads. **People started pushing and kicking, and it wasn't safe at all. Over a hundred students, standing near a bus stop on a pavement that was maybe four metres wide.** People started spitting, things were getting thrown, and just before it got worse, **someone shouted out, 'Pigs!', meaning the police.**

It wasn't one police car; there were four or five police vans and cars. **It was time to cut and do a runner.** In all the chaos, me and the boy managed to lock eyes one more time, and then lost one another. **I was busy focusing on not getting caught, getting rid of my weapons and getting home.**

I turned straight down Church Street and slipped one tool into the drain. The other two I threw under a stall selling fruits. I then quickly took my blazer and shirt off, shoved them into my bag, and noticed a family standing in the market. The mum was looking at shoes and the two kids were waiting with bags in their hands. **I stood as close to them**

as possible to give the impression that I was with them. I started to look at the shoes too but kept an eye on kids from my school getting chased by the police. **I stayed calm, stayed in character and watched the police run straight past me.**

Then I slipped away, making my way home slowly. **It felt like one of the longest walks home I'd ever taken.** I was still on edge, wondering if those guys were still around or planning to jump me. **Sirens wailed in the distance** and one police car even drove past me, but I focused on getting home, trying my hardest to look casual, **like nothing had happened**.

Arriving at the bottom of my block of flats, I took a deep breath, composed myself and opened my front door. **Suddenly I felt safe**. I said, 'As salaam alaykum,' to my parents, **which in Arabic means 'peace be with you'**. It's how we greet each other. I got changed, prayed, had a bowl of cereal and chilled with the family. None of them knew the mess I had just been involved in. **None of them knew about this double life I was living.**

For now, I focused on the peace and safety I had at home with my family. Literally just being in the living room, parents cuddled up on the sofa, a good movie on with snacks at the ready. **This was life.**

Back then, we didn't have smartphones. We had something called MSN, which was an online messenger on your computer. When I went on it that night, the chats were blowing up.

Everyone was talking about what happened and who had got caught. For those who had been there just to watch, it was all exciting. But none of them knew how terrifying it had been for me, because my life had actually been at risk. I couldn't fall asleep easily that night. I wondered if I should have started the fight, but what would have happened to me or anybody else?

A SENSE OF BELONGING

The next day, people were already asking if there was going to be a part two. And although one part of me **felt like a coward** because I didn't start the fight, everyone **showed me respect**, saying that I wasn't scared to stand in front of all those people. **The truth is I was scared, and I was only there because I wasn't alone!**

But I didn't tell them this. **I accepted the attention that I got.** I even felt good about how it seemed to bring me and the guys together even more – we had a tighter connection. **If someone agreed to back you in a fight, it was one of the most loyal things they could do**, and so now I made sure that my guys knew if they ever got into any beef that I would be there for them as well.

This was important because at this age, I had friends from different areas, and I would often go to those areas, or they would come to mine. People were starting to get moved to, mostly getting *ROBBED* for phones or money, and so going out alone wasn't ideal. I knew people who were **ROBBED** for their trainers and bikes, and one guy was even beaten up badly because he had nothing of value that the people could rob from him! **We would roll around in groups. We had no choice because numbers meant something, but more important was the sense of belonging.**

One day I was out with my boys, and we were in an area called Queensway, which wasn't far from where I lived. It was a hotspot to go grab a quick Nando's, go to the arcade and try to find some new girls to talk to. On this particular day, there were a lot more people out. There was apparently going to be a **big clash between two gangs**, the Kosovans and the Somalis.

We didn't want any part of it, so we decided to leave. But as we left, police vans arrived, and they weren't playing around. Everyone starting scattering, some got caught, but me and my guys got away. **We were calm because we knew we weren't involved.**

We were walking to get the bus home, and as we approached the bus stop, a police van pulled up. One of my guys started running, and then the other one. **I stood there because I had no reason to run.** The police held my arms, asked me where I had just come from. They emptied my pockets and searched me, all while my friends were watching from a distance. **They were close enough to see what was happening, but far enough away to escape if an officer tried to chase them.**

Apparently I matched the description of someone selling drugs *(wasn't the first time I'd heard this)*, and so they forced my arms behind my back and threw me into the van. I knew this was a lie, because at first they were suggesting that I was part of the big fight that had just happened, and now, for no reason, they used unnecessary force to put my arms behind me and to literally throw me into the van.

This was the first time I had ever been in the back of a police van. I was annoyed, and my arm was a little hurt, but it was situations like this that brought me and my friends closer. We were in it together. Well, that's what I thought. But when I deeped it . . .

I WAS THE ONLY ONE IN THE BACK OF A POLICE VAN, BEING DRIVEN TO A POLICE STATION WITH HANDCUFFS ON THAT WERE CUTTING INTO MY WRISTS.

The police put me in a cell and I saw the names of guys I knew written on the wall. **I just wanted to leave. It was late, I was hungry.** Then they came back and asked me where I got my phone from. Now they were holding me on suspicion of theft because my phone had been reported stolen some time ago. **I had bought it second hand; I didn't know if the person who sold it to me stole it or not.** They told me they had to officially interview me about this and that they had to invite one of my parents in because of my age. **NOW I WAS SCARED!**

I knew I didn't want my mum coming as she would panic, so I gave them my dad's number, but I was afraid. **It was late, he was probably sleeping, and**

I knew he wouldn't be happy. He got to the police station and didn't look at me once. We did the interview. I told them the truth about everything and how I was being held for no reason.
My dad also gave them a word about profiling and abusing power.

Although he was angry at me, he also defended me, saying to them: 'Out of all the guys out there, you arrest my son?' He mentioned he had just driven past a number of young guys who were not Black and clearly selling drugs on his way to the police station. **He questioned them about their morals in such a calm and articulate way that the interview was terminated more quickly.** They let me go. My dad still didn't look at me, which kind of hurt me. **He told me he was disappointed and said that I could make my own way home.**

This was the first time I felt disconnected from my dad, and I didn't like it. I was annoyed because I genuinely didn't do anything wrong that night. **But I also knew I had been out late and would often get up to no good.** I had spent so many years of my life doing what I could to impress him, to get his approval and to build on our connection,

93

but now I saw how things that may have made me look cool to others would damage the love and connection I had with family.

My father had always been there for me, so he also didn't deserve for me to bring trouble his way. **It's all I kept thinking about on my walk home.**

INVEST IN REAL CONNECTIONS

When I look back at the things I did as a teenager, it really confirms my belief there is a God, **because I got into some situations that could have ended very badly**. I also understand that some people reading this might be excited by the story I just told, while others would have hated to be involved in those situations.

Let me tell you something: there's nothing exciting about it. My life could have ended on multiple occasions if things had gone a different way. **Doing foolish things to build connections with others isn't smart.** I wish I'd been able to **say no**, and not succumb to the **peer pressure**. Sometimes we put pressure on ourselves too. I definitely did. I often felt like I had to make an impression or that I needed to do certain things to get the validation of others.

WHY DID I DO THIS?

I can see now that one of our biggest fears as humans is that we won't be loved, **and this is why we do things to impress others even if we don't want to do them**. I wish I'd known that **saying no is a strength, NOT a weakness**.

WANTING TO BE LOVED AND BELONG IS A CORE DRIVER OF HUMAN BEHAVIOUR, ONE THAT WE SEARCH FOR IN EVERY AREA OF OUR LIVES.

This first starts with our own families and carers. As we grow up, our relationships with them can begin to change. **We might start to feel like we can't share everything with them**, that they don't understand us or what we're going through, and so we create a division or a disconnect. This can make us place more importance on the relationships and connections we experience with others outside of our home. Friends who we can share our experiences with, be open around without judgement, **and they somehow become our family away from home**. Remember, you can't choose your family, but you can choose your friends and who you hang around with.

Although most people claim to be open-minded nowadays, **the truth is that people like people who are like them**. It doesn't mean you don't like other types of people; it just means you like people who are like you. Maybe they have the same hobbies, they have the same faith, they like the same artists. **People look for commonalities to form a sense of belonging.** Think about it: on your first day in a new school or at a club, didn't you first look for someone who looked like you? Maybe you even went and sat next to them because it made you feel safe. **That's the importance of belonging and how connection drives part of the decisions we make.**

Now imagine how important having friends outside of the house is to young people who don't have families, or families who aren't present. This is the case for many people out there. It might be for you too. So, without even acknowledging it, if you wake up and there is an adult in the house who loves you and cares about you, that's a blessing that many young people don't get to experience.

If in your situation, things at home aren't great with your parents or siblings, or both, I can only imagine how difficult that must feel. There can be several reasons why this is, but let me share something with you that took me many years to understand: **people are doing the best they can with the best they've got.** No one's parents, family or carers are perfect. They are also people who are just trying to do their best, and like you, **at some point they make mistakes.** With that said, not every relation is the same.

For example, **only now as adults** do me and my brother have a level of brotherhood where we have healthy conversations, use the words **'I LOVE YOU'** towards each other and see eye to eye. For many years we weren't in each other's lives; we were around but there was very little connection there. Whereas I know some brothers who have been best friends forever. Same relation, just different behaviour, **and that's OK**.

I remember back in school there were some guys I knew who seemed to always be angry. They had very bad social behaviour and didn't do great in school. These guys enjoyed inflicting pain on others, and even when they did get into a relationship, they didn't know how to be affectionate. **When I spoke to them, I discovered the type of upbringing they had, and everything clicked.** All that anger, all that bad behaviour, was because they were looking for love and a sense of belonging, **but they hadn't had those relationships at home**. They learned to put up barriers to strangers, to not let people get too close because the feeling was unfamiliar. **But what they feared was not being loved or being hurt.**

Though I'd had a secure upbringing, I was also willing to get into fights where most people carried knives, **put my life at risk, put my future at risk, all because I wanted to feel connected to others** and to be good enough. **But it's not what we do that matters most, it's *why* we do what we do.** The truth is, I wanted love and belonging. Being respected, having a tight crew and proving myself in a fight made me feel that way, and so these things became part of my life.

DOSAGE: Oxytocin

There is a neurotransmitter and hormone in your body called oxytocin, which pays a huge role in your life and interacts with your need for love and belonging.

You know when you're having a bad day, or someone has made you upset or angry, **and then you hug someone and that feeling starts fading away?** That's because this chemical called **OXYTOCIN** is being released.

You also get oxytocin when you shake a friend's hand, fist bump, get bro hug, get your hair done by your friend or, check this out, even if you see someone doing a nice thing for someone else.

Think about those scenes in movies when the man is waiting for his wife to arrive: he's holding flowers in his hands, his shoulders are slumped because she's late, **but then she appears in the distance.**

Her eyes are shining with excitement, smile beaming with love, which makes him breathe deep and smile back. Just seeing someone we love and are connected to triggers oxytocin. But there are other things that trigger it too, **including when we cuddle a pet, listen to music or spend time with people we trust**. And like **SEROTONIN, OXYTOCIN** can be released when we're on social media. When we have a positive interaction online or share words of support, **oxytocin is released**.

Why am I sharing this with you? **Because as you've read, it's possible to experience these chemicals and needs in both good and harmful ways.** The truth is, **I DIDN'T NEED TO GET INTO FIGHTS TO FEEL MORE CONNECTED TO OTHERS AROUND ME**. Maybe all I needed was to hug my family more, cuddle my pet or spend time with **real friends** who liked me for being me, not for someone I was pretending to be.

REAL CONNECTION

THE WAY WE CONNECT HAS CHANGED A LOT IN THE LAST TWENTY YEARS. SOCIAL CONNECTION IS NOW SOCIAL MEDIA CONNECTION. WE HAVE TRADED A LOT OF HUMAN CONNECTION FOR ONLINE FRIENDSHIPS AND STRANGERS WHO WE FOLLOW BECAUSE WE THINK THEIR LIFE LOOKS COOL OR ASPIRATIONAL. BUT SOME OF THE PEOPLE WE SEE ONLINE, WITH THE BIGGEST FOLLOWINGS AND CONNECTIONS, ARE THE MOST LONELY AND INSECURE PEOPLE.

Isolation is a form of torture, but because devices and **SOCIAL MEDIA** give you the **ILLUSION** of being in a room full of friends, you might feel happy to spend days by yourself in your room with your online community. **But this isn't the same as spending quality time with friends and family.** How you use your smartphone and what you do with it will be personal to you. **Your habits are formed by things you think give you pleasure, and so you keep repeating them.** The more you are on your phone, the less human interaction you are having, **the**

harder it is to make friends in person and the more difficult you will find it to connect with people offline.

REAL LIFE IS WHERE TRUE CONNECTION LIES. So how do you find friendships and relationships that are **meaningful and healthy?** This is something I found really hard to figure out over the years. But eventually I realised I needed to think about what **common ground** I was basing my connection with someone on. **Was it something good or something harmful?** For example, perhaps you play sport with someone but you also share a love for music — this will help you form a deeper connection with that person. Whereas I have coached addicts who have said their best friends are also addicts — **they connected because of their addiction and that made their bad habits more engrained.**

Next, I had to think about *why* I was connecting with someone. Sometimes we search for connection with the wrong people in the wrong ways. Just like I did with the boys at school. **This is where making better decisions come into place.** One question you can ask yourself is this: **'Is doing this thing going to support me or cause**

problems long term?' Be **STRONG ENOUGH** to walk alone in the **RIGHT DIRECTION**, rather than get lost in a group walking in the **WRONG DIRECTION**. I use the word **STRONG** because **following the crowd is easy**. Making a decision based on what is **BEST FOR YOU** can sometimes be challenging, but as I eventually realised, **it's your decisions**, not your conditions, **that determine your destiny**. Your friends and your family won't always like or agree with your decisions, **but if those decisions move you more towards the future you want, then that is a brave step worth making**.

WE ALL MAKE MISTAKES. We all make the wrong decisions. And we all succumb to peer pressure. That's the nature of the journey we're all on, especially when we're young. But the truth is that **we know deep down when we shouldn't do something**. We've all been in situations where our friends are doing something, and we really don't want to do it, but because they keep insisting, **it overpowers our gut feeling that we don't want to take part**.

ALWAYS TRUST YOUR INSTINCT. You might think saying **'NO'** or making an excuse is going to alienate you from the group, **but it's the stronger move. You might even be respected more for it.**

That's how you're going to see **who your real friends are**. And if they're not cool with it, there are millions of other people you can make friends with.

Don't be scared to change your circle of friends if you feel your current ones aren't a good influence on you. I've done this. Yes, at times it hurt, it was lonely, I missed them. But I saw the long-term benefit of updating my circle.

Let's have a go . . . Grab a piece of paper and draw a large circle like the one below. Write down all the names of people you consider to be your friends.

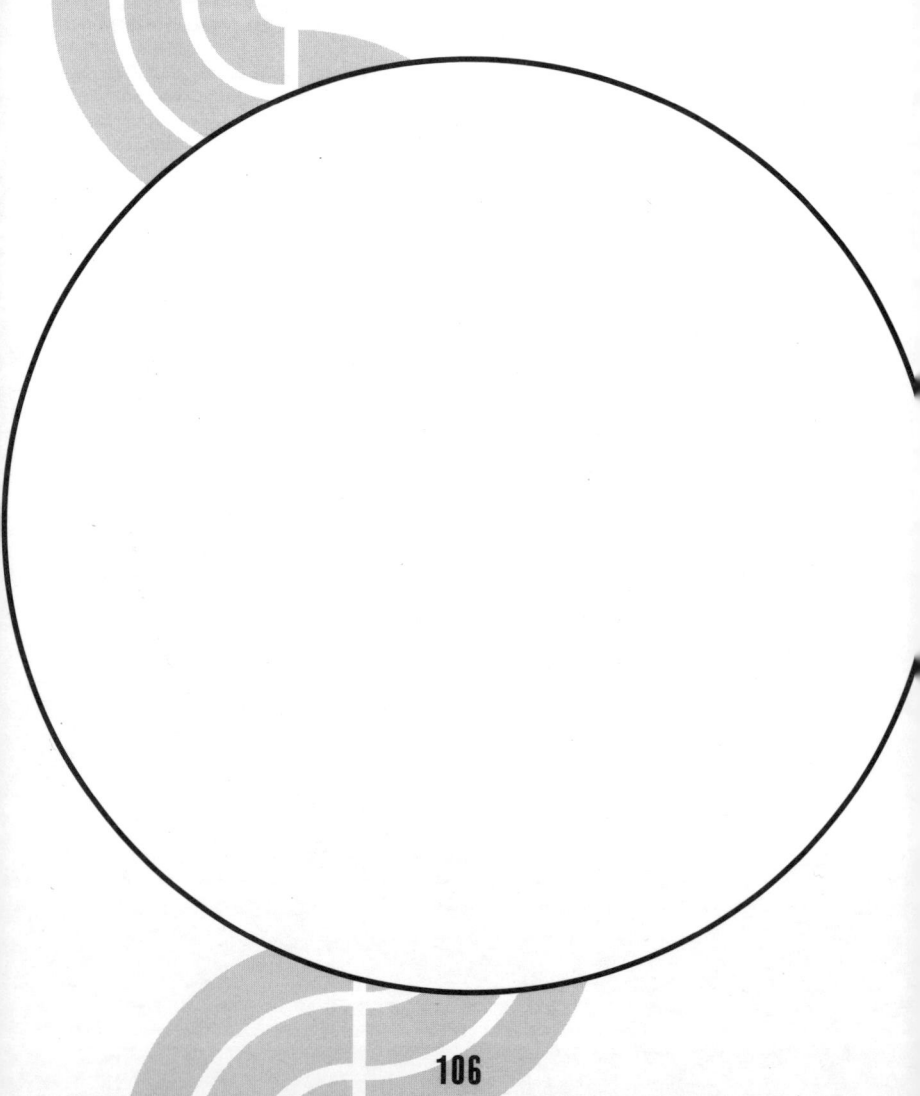

Now draw a medium circle. I want you to look at the names in the first circle and only write their names in the second circle if you feel **that friend respects you and is someone you like having around you**. Really think about it.

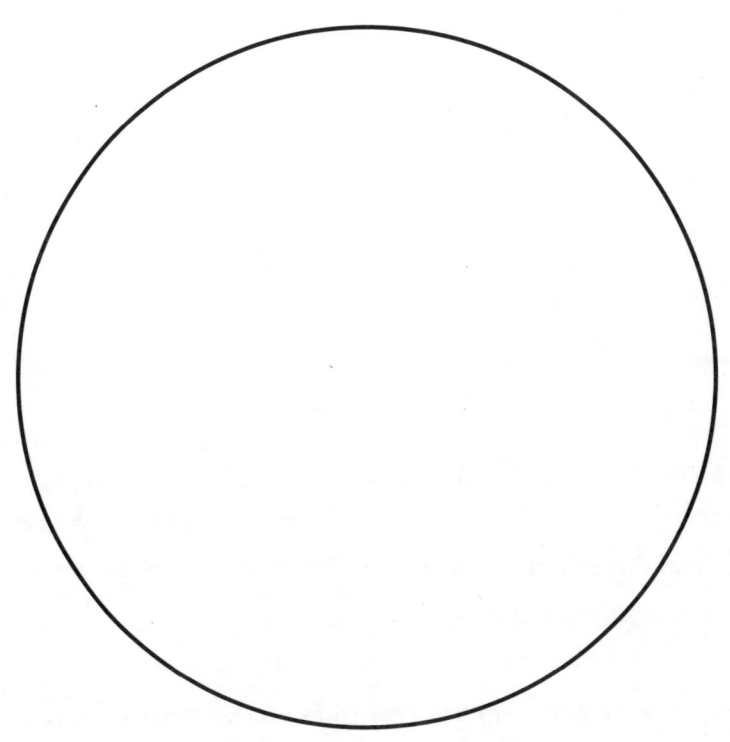

Amazing. Now, draw a smaller circle. I want you to write only the names of those who you **truly feel are amazing friends, who you can trust with your life** and who would support you if you ever wanted to do something that you felt was best for you and not what they wanted. **Consider whether or not they would put you in this circle too.**

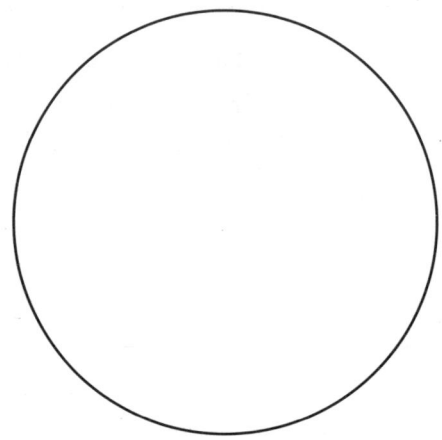

As the circles have got smaller, I am guessing your list of friends has too. **This is actually a good thing! These are your true friends, who you can have quality friendships with.**

'A few trustworthy friends hold more value than many superficial relationships'
- Sheikh Nazim

Nurture those friends in the small circle. Those are the friendships you want to protect, that will offer you connection and belonging, and **not force you to do things you don't want to**.

If something serious had happened to me back when I was a teenager, this book you're reading now might not even exist. **That's how important making the right decisions is, and this includes decisions about the kind of friends you make** and the things you get up to together, which is exactly what the next chapter is about.

CHAPTER 3

RESPECT - AND WHERE TO FIND IT

I WAS FIFTEEN YEARS OLD WHEN I FIRST SAW A KNIFE ENTER SOMEONE'S BODY.

By this point, I was at a different school. My old school had politely transferred me to another one because of bad behaviour. **In other words, they kicked me out.** This was an inner-city London school — the playgrounds were basic, they didn't have grass, there were faint paint marks outlining the borders of the football pitches and they had tall, grey wired gates **to keep us from climbing out**.

It was lunchtime. I was standing in the middle of the playground and all I could think was that I felt like I was in a movie scene. **In front of me there was a guy getting his head kicked in** on the ground by someone wearing black Timberland boots. To my left was **another guy curled in a ball getting whacked with the end of a belt**. And to my right, a **guy had just been stabbed in his back**. The knife was still there, but he was standing and swinging punches, almost oblivious to it.

This was one of the biggest racial fights I had seen yet. It was Black kids against Kurdish kids, and I felt torn because I considered them both to be my brothers. Even in the chaos, I saw some of the Kurdish kids look at me, ready to attack. Then when they realised it was me, they moved on to find the next Black person.

I couldn't believe this was happening around me. I couldn't believe it was happening at school. And I couldn't believe it was happening between guys who would have to sit in the same tutor groups together a few hours later.

I couldn't stand and watch it anymore, so **I started trying to break up the fights**. I pushed people off each other. I grabbed belts out of people's hands and kept shouting for everyone to **calm down**.

Here's the big difference I noticed going from being a fourteen-year-old to a fifteen-year-old. When we were fourteen, **someone might carry a weapon to a fight, but would normally just end up in a fist fight**. The worst you'd get was a black eye, busted lip or bruises. The knife or weapon was purely to build more fear in the other person. **But somehow, within the space of a year, people started using the knives.** So now people were getting into fights knowing that . . .

THEY COULD GET STABBED.

What did this mean? More people started carrying blades or stashing them in places nearby. At this time, knives weren't hard to find or buy — people would steal them from the shop, buy them from market stalls without being asked for ID and even ask local drug addicts to find some for a small payment.

The first time I carried a knife, I was going to play basketball with friends. **It felt weird.** I was just out to play a sport with my friends but was also carrying this thing with me in case we got into a fight. **It didn't feel right, but, if I'm being honest with you, at the time it also felt a little bit gangster.** I never carried the knife to hurt someone else, but I thought it would protect me if someone tried to stab me. **It was a strange concept to understand.** I was now older and bigger, **but that didn't mean anything on road**. On road you've got elders to deal with, other boys from different blocks and kids from different schools. I still felt like a soft boy at my core, **but I also felt like I needed to be road ready, mentally prepared for anything**.

At home, I would stand in front of the mirror with a bandana covering my face, topless while wielding two kitchen knives in my hand. **I used to pretend I was talking to people and acting the part I thought I was meant to play**, while pointing the knives into the mirror as if I was pointing them at someone.

I'd noticed when I watched my brother fight, or other guys who looked like they were enjoying it, that they all had this particular look in their eyes. **So I tried to replicate that look.** It wasn't easy. I even asked my sister to help me pose for photos that made me look hard. I used these for my MSN display pictures, and when people commented on them, it boosted my self-belief, **but I knew inside I was acting**. Sure, I could think about hurting people when I was in a state of anger — that wasn't hard at all. **What I struggled with was understanding how these people had this way of thinking long-term.**

Were they angry all the time? How did they have so much hate in their hearts for so long?

I started listening to as much gangster rap as possible and I played *GTA San Andreas* daily because that was all about **GANGS, VIOLENCE, WINNING**. I fell in love with playing fighting games like *Fight Night*, thinking it would help me learn to fight and to protect myself. **I thought perhaps I could brainwash myself to finally become this hard guy.** But none of this mattered unless I could test it out in the real world. **And that was my next task.**

One day in school, there was going to be a fight between my friend and another guy. **I didn't like the other guy because he had immediately become a threat when he joined my school the year before.** Back then, rumours had gone round that he'd been trying to chat up my girlfriend and that he'd said he could take her from me. **Now, in school no one ever fact checked. If a rumour went around it had to be true**, although no one could point out who said it or verify its authenticity. People kept telling me, 'This guy is taking your girl,' and I felt like I had to prove myself.

I had to show him who I was in this school.

I took my blazer off, rolled up my sleeves and went looking for him. People started following me. I couldn't find him and then someone told me he was in the playground talking to my girlfriend right at that moment. **I LOST IT.** I started running. I got outside and panned around for him. **I sprinted towards him, not quite sure of what I was going to do.** He was walking with my girlfriend and two other girls, his back towards me. As I got close, **I launched into the air, bent my knee to my chest and kicked him over from behind**. He fell to the ground, got up, shocked, and **I confronted him** about what he was playing at. He said he and my girlfriend were just friends. She said the same.

At this point, this was all I wanted to hear. But I didn't know what to do. I wasn't angry anymore, but I couldn't let people think that was it, so I kept running my mouth, making sure he knew that this could have escalated.

Fast-forward a year, and this guy and my friend were going to fight. My friend asked me if I would back him and straight away, **I said yes**. The plan was to walk to a nearby car park after school, **no weapons allowed**.

They squared up to each other. No one was making the first move. I stood behind the guy and so, when my friend nodded, **I grabbed the boy's arms so my friend could land a couple of shots at him**. But out of nowhere someone landed a punch on my face from behind me. **I DESERVED IT, BUT I FLIPPED OUT.**

I started almost skipping around the car park, unbuttoning my shirt, shouting with my crazy eyes on, spit dripping from my lips until one of my guys pulled me aside and said, 'FAM, CALM IT.' I had respect for this guy, and so I started to calm myself down. **He said that the guy who punched me had also pulled out a knife to stab me**, but my friend pulled him away and convinced him not to. My friend knew him from his area; he was older than us. I didn't even know what had happened in the fight between those two guys. **All I kept thinking about was that I was almost stabbed.**

I felt guilty for holding the guy's arms behind his back and it had almost cost me a heavy price. But, even worse, the next day in school everyone was talking about how Omar got **SPARKED** (punched) and that the guy got away with it. Again, because I cared what people thought, **I cared about my 'reputation', I felt like I had to retaliate**. Even though I'd nearly been stabbed for the first time.

I told some guys, 'After school we are going looking for him.' This was one of the most **STUPID** things I ever did, because not only was I going after someone who was older than me, **but he was also capable of stabbing me** — and now I had the grand idea of walking into his ends. **This would be the definition of getting caught slipping.**

I got some guys together, then I went home, grabbed what I needed to grab, and we caught the bus to where we knew he hung out. One thing I noticed about myself was that I was either black or white —

there was no grey area with me. I either didn't do something at all, or I did it in the extreme. It was the same with my emotions. When I got sad, I was really sad. When I got angry, I switched completely. **I didn't know how to regulate those emotions.** Because I felt like this older guy had disrespected me, **my ego was hurt**, the facade I had created was being questioned, and **I couldn't deal with it**.

We jumped off the bus, and already I felt uneasy. This was unknown territory to me and I was in a place I actually didn't want to be. It wasn't an area you came to looking for trouble, **but somehow this was apparently something I had to do**. Another friend met us at the bus stop with his Rottweiler. We walked around, popped our heads into barber shops, chicken shops, but we couldn't find him. We were also aware that there weren't many of us, **and that at any moment a larger group could randomly be out and catch us slipping**.

Inside, I was praying that I wouldn't actually find him, but on the outside, I wanted it to look like I was on the hunt. I could see that the guys with me thought I was brave, going after someone who was at least three years older, which is a huge deal. **Everything I was doing was for show, to get respect — it wasn't for me.**

We didn't find him, and we decided to leave it. **Once I had calmed down, I was relieved.** I only hoped he wouldn't find out I'd come looking for him, **because I knew he would come straight for me . . .**

HUSTLING

When I was moved from my old school to my new school, it was tough. **There was a lot of beef between the schools.** Most of the guys from my new school came from different areas, which meant **I was slipping again**. I did start to make new friends and I built a good reputation. I was still one of the fastest runners, and I was the best dancer in the school. **But I felt like I was missing something — money.** Some of the other guys always had the latest trainers, started buying LV belts and wore big-brand jackets to school. **I WAS ENVIOUS AND CURIOUS.** I wanted to wear brand names like that, brands that would impress. **I just knew I didn't have that kind of money.**

SO I STARTED UP A SWEET ENTERPRISE. I would buy sweets, crisps, chocolates and drinks at wholesale and bring them into school to sell, and they sold. **I was a natural salesman, just like my dad.** But I wanted to earn more. Realising I needed to push it harder, I got one young kid from each of the years below me and gave each of them a number of products to sell every day for some money in return. **These guys were hustlers!** Sometimes they would come to me before the day was finished, asking me if I had more to sell, and then I realised I had to have stock. I had a supply problem. **I convinced a few kids in the school to let me use their lockers so that I could store more products.**

It was an exciting operation. People started asking me if I could get other products and I did my best to deliver. I was making a good amount of money per week, **but I knew it wasn't the same type of money some of the other guys were making**, so I started to think about what else I could sell in school. My father had some stock from a cosmetics business he had — bottles of perfume, eyeliner, lip pencils, etc. — and was happy to let me sell them. This was better because it meant that I made more profit on selling one product rather than selling lots of sweets or crisps. **So I slowed down the confectionary enterprise and opened up a mini department store in school.**

People were buying, even the teachers! I was cheaper than Superdrug, and kids were even bringing their parents to buy from me after school. **Now, yes, my focus was on making money, but that didn't mean I didn't study.** I really enjoyed my lessons. My father always said, 'classroom for learning, playground for playing,' and I adopted that mindset.

Over time, I made some money and bought some tracksuits, trainers, a new phone and more. **But I still wasn't as cool as the other guys.** Splashing out £300 on a Gucci belt still felt like a lot to me when I knew I could use that same £300 and turn it into £600 with profit. But the other guys seemed more desirable, dangerous and intriguing to girls. **The older guys had the clothes, bling, cars, girls and, most of all, respect.**

They had a lifestyle that all of us youngers looked at and admired. They were our inspiration, and I realised that if I wanted that lifestyle then I had to do what they were doing to get there. **This is what led me down a very dark path . . .**

GET OUT WHILE YOU CAN

Before I knew it, I was approached just outside of my school by someone who said, 'I HEARD THAT YOU'RE THE CANDY MAN, YEAH?' I didn't know who this guy was, but **HE DIDN'T LOOK LIKE SOMEONE I WANTED TO BE RUDE TO.** He told me to come and sit in his car, and I was already impressed. I had never sat in an Audi Sport car before. **This guy had piles of money stashed at the front and I already knew he was someone serious.** He was very direct. Asked me how much money I made selling sweets and beauty stuff. He was impressed and said he'd take me for some food before we spoke business. We approached the place, and when people opened the door for him and welcomed him, I thought, **Wow, this guy has respect**. I had a sandwich and a slice of cheesecake – the cheesecake was, like, £7! My head was still confused because I knew I could get a whole vanilla cheesecake from Sainsbury's for £2.

He told me he liked me because I was '**DIFFERENT**'. He said he could tell I was smart and he could help me make some **REAL MONEY**. I sat and listened to him talk. I observed everything about him, how everything he wore was designer, how he had spoken to and agreed to meet two different girls that day. I thought to myself:

I WANT TO BE LIKE THIS GUY!

He paid for the food, stopped a black cab and told me to go wherever I needed to go. **He gave me one £50 note to pay the driver, then threw me another £50 note and told me to keep it.** I waited until he left in his car, then I jumped out of the cab and said, 'Sorry, I can walk from here,' **just so I could keep more of the money**.

I was torn because I was scared of my parents, and I didn't want to let them down. I also knew some people who had family and friends who got into mad trouble from getting involved with drugs, **and I saw how it affected their families**. I knew if I did get involved that I would be doing it to make a name for myself, and to make some serious bread, **BUT SO MANY OF THE GUYS SAID THAT ONCE YOU'RE IN THEN YOU'RE IN, AND THAT'S THE PART THAT SCARED ME**.

Some time went by and I was wondering when that guy would come to see me again. I didn't know his name and I didn't tell anyone about it. **But eventually, I recognised his car outside of my school one day, and he told me he had some work for me.** Half an hour later I was sitting in a kitchen and on the table in front of me were **BAGS OF WEED**. The guy told me to get them bagged up into smaller bags, each weighing exactly a certain number of grams. He said that I needed to get it done by 8 p.m. I knew I could get it done much sooner so I put on a pair of latex gloves and got to work.

I played some music from my phone and got to it. Before I knew it I had already finished the first bag. There were still two more to go. The guy wasn't in the house the whole time. I didn't make it my business to watch what he was doing; **I just wanted to make a good impression.** I split up the tasks and found my own system, so that I finished way before 8 p.m.

The guy came back in the late afternoon, and I was sitting watching TV. His first reaction was, 'Yo, what do you think you're doing, fam? There's work to be done.' I told him I'd finished. He looked surprised. He went into the kitchen and looked around. **He asked whether I did it all by myself.** Then he pulled out three or four random packets from each bag and **told me that I'd better hope these all weighed the correct amount**. They all did.

He looked at me, smiled, gave me a little side hug and said, 'You're a little G, innit.' **I felt happy that he was pleased with my work.** He called someone up and I could hear him telling the guy how much work I was able to get done.

He said that I could go home and gave me some money. But I gave him the money back and said I didn't want to get paid for today. I said for me it was a trial day – I wanted to make sure I was good at it first and he could pay me properly next time. **I thought this would build trust, but he flipped!**

He told me to open my bag now. He told me to empty my pockets. He even told me to take my clothes off. He thought I didn't want the money because I had stolen some of the weed. I told him, 'I've never even tried it!' I even showed him a box where I put all of the stem parts, which I didn't think would be fair to put into bags.

ON ROAD, TRUST WAS EVERYTHING. THE PROBLEM WAS THAT WITH THIS LIFESTYLE, IT'S DOG EAT DOG. YOU NEVER KNOW WHO'S GOING TO SNAKE YOU.

I told him that when I had guys selling sweets for me, they had at least two days to prove they could do it before getting paid, and I was under the same impression here. This made him loosen up.

He gave me a little black phone and said he'd text me when work was available, and that when he texted, I'd better make moves quick.

On the bus home I felt proud of myself. I wanted to tell someone about it, but when I thought about it, there wasn't really anyone I could tell. Some of my friends would judge me and my family would kill me, so I kept it to myself.

The guy texted me once every couple of weeks. Same place, same time, same routine. **And it felt good to have some money in my pocket**, to wear new shoes to school, to have the latest Nike backpack. It wasn't a crazy amount of money, but for a short while, I felt invincible.

Many other kids did too. **They aspired to be big-time gangsters and olders like the guy I was working for.** But as time went on and I saw what kind of lifestyle it was, I started wanting less and less to do with it. **Then I got a text on that little black phone in the morning on a school day,** which I thought was a mistake. So I ignored it and went to school as normal. That was the mistake . . . After school, he was waiting for me. I got in his car, and he grabbed my jaw and pressed my head against the window, saying, **'I TOLD YOU: WHEN I TEXT YOU, YOU COME.'**

I protested that I never missed school, and he said I'd better be prepared to miss anything. There was real anger in his eyes and I could suddenly see how dangerous he really was. I knew in the back of my mind that I needed to step away when I could. **Deep down, I knew I was a smart guy.** I didn't know what I wanted to do, but I enjoyed buying and selling, and I was getting good grades. **I had been flattered when he'd approached me and I thought it might boost my rep.** But I didn't want to be a foot soldier.

This is what other kids at school were doing. They were meeting the buyers face to face, plotting on the block, **getting into police chases.**

This wasn't a life I wanted. There was too much risk and danger. And things could escalate quickly. I was sixteen years old the first time someone I knew at school was stabbed and killed. This was a year after I saw that other guy get stabbed in his back and keep on fighting - luckily, he had survived.

I had heard of other people from different areas being killed, **but this was the first time it happened to someone I knew**. Some say it was an accident; his neck was sliced and he bled out. He was in the year below me and was someone I had prayed next to a couple of times at Friday prayer in school, had kicked around playing football with and would talk to from time to time. **It was another one of my friends who had done it, and, of course, he ended up going to prison. One life lost and another ruined.**

I remember that feeling in school of someone suddenly just not being there anymore. I didn't know the guy who'd died so well, **but it was still devastating**. At a gathering, his closer friends shared stories about him and what they would miss.

No one mentioned any of the designer clothes he wore or any cool things that he had. **They spoke about his character and the loyal friend that he was.**

All those things I placed significance on, at the end of the day, were insignificant. I had wanted to have the expensive things so that I could get recognition. I had wanted people to look at me and see that I was doing well. **I was even risking putting myself in dangerous situations to get it. And when it boiled down to it, all of those things really meant nothing at all.**

SHINE IN YOUR OWN WAY

Everyone wants to feel seen, be special and have the respect of others. What we're looking for is significance, but how we get it differs from person to person. **When you grow up feeling insignificant** like I did, you automatically crave the opposite. Looking back at my younger self, **I see a boy desperate to be seen, heard and respected**. Navigating a world where violence, status and material possessions seemed to define one's worth, it took me years to understand that these were hollow markers of status and there are other more worthwhile ways to find it.

We all seek recognition and a sense of worth – whether it's excelling in academics, being good at sport, building friendships, or, as in my case, a misguided pursuit of respect in a violent environment.

The need to feel significant is deeply ingrained in our psyche. It gives us a sense of purpose and identity. But the way we seek it can either build us up or tear us down.

When I was growing up, wearing the latest trainers or having the most expensive belt was a status symbol, a way to show the world that you mattered. **But the satisfaction it brought was always short-lived.** There was always someone with a newer pair of trainers or a more expensive belt, and so **the cycle never ended**. My pursuit of those things led me down a dark road, and my early experiences taught me harsh lessons about the dangers of **seeking significance in the wrong places**. Carrying a knife and getting involved in violent altercations was a **misguided attempt to earn respect and feel a sense of importance**. These actions didn't lead to true significance; **they only brought fear, isolation and danger**.

Hustling at school by selling sweets and cosmetics gave me a temporary sense of accomplishment and respect from my peers. **It felt good to be recognised for my entrepreneurial skills,** and in many ways, I was using my brain to make money. **Having a side hustle or earning some extra cash isn't a bad thing**

in itself, if you're doing it for the right reasons. But mine was a fragile form of significance. It relied on the need for external validation and material success, **which are both fleeting**. Striving for expensive clothes, flashy cars and public accolades can give you a temporary boost, **but these things often leave a lingering emptiness because they depend on others' opinions**.

What I soon realised was that **true significance is not about what we own or how others perceive us. It's about the impact we have on the world and the people around us.** It's about our character, our kindness and our ability to stand up for what is right. The people who truly matter in our lives are those who **see beyond the surface and value us for who we are**, not what we have. Don't get me wrong, I still like nice things. But I am not driven by them anymore, and I don't seek them for the external validation of others. It's another one of those **breakthrough moments** when we're able to recognise this and then act on it.

I realised true wealth isn't just about money; it's about our quality of life, the people we have around us, the emotions we feel on a day-to-day basis. It's about living a life that has meaning. **If you look for inward-driven significance, you will find more fulfilment and self-satisfaction.** For example, when I do my five daily prayers, most of the time no one else sees me, **but I feel significant because I know I did them and how they benefit me**. Similarly, I have bought food for homeless people and left it beside them as they sleep, not needing them to know it was me who gave it to them. **These acts bring a sense of inner peace that external validation can never match.**

THE SOURCE OF YOUR SIGNIFICANCE

I want you to think about something: **How can you go about meeting your fundamental need for significance?**

A heavyweight boxing champion wants to win the belt for significance, while even a monk or Sufi who is looking for spiritual enlightenment **is looking for significance**. Walking into a fight with my boys behind me made me feel significant. Being selected by someone older to do work for them made me feel significant.

BUT I WAS FINDING SIGNIFICANCE IN THE WRONG PLACES.

As with everything that drives our behaviour, **we can seek significance both constructively and destructively**. Some people assert their significance by raising their voices the loudest in arguments, dominating the conversation to make themselves feel more important. If you have a friend who finds it amusing to get in trouble in class, they're also seeking significance. **Their actions are a way to gain attention and recognition, even if it's negative.** Others people find significance by belittling others. They get a sense of power and importance from making others feel inferior. **These people are also known as haters. In my experience, when you show them that what they say doesn't bother you, that's how you win. Don't take it personally.**

But there are positive ways to find significance. Excelling in school or sport can provide a strong sense of significance. Acts of kindness, like volunteering or helping friends, can also achieve this feeling — **they create lasting fulfilment because they positively impact others and foster a sense of community.** And creative activities like art, music, dance, film-making or writing can allow you to **EXPRESS YOURSELF**. This can also help with other challenges you might be facing. For example, I often found myself **struggling with anger** and not knowing what to do with my emotions, but dance helped me with this — **I could express myself and channel my emotions into something creative.**

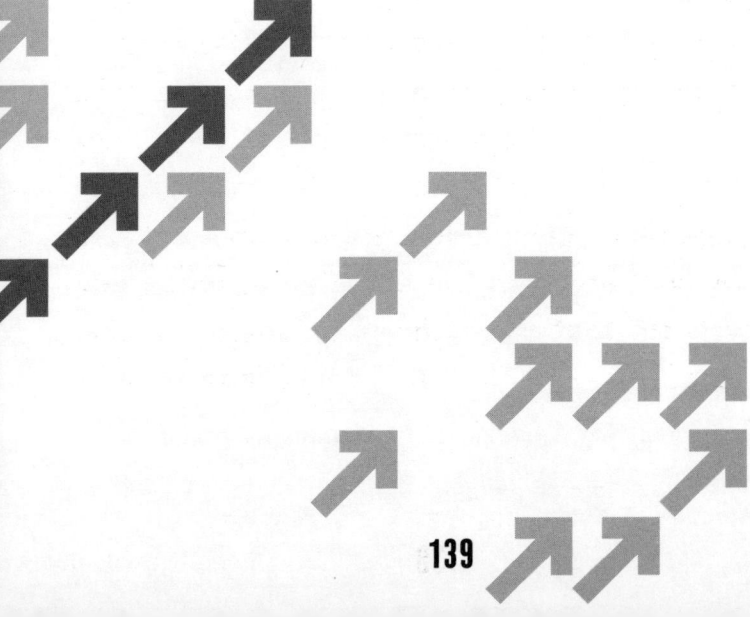

DOSAGE: Serotonin

What about the ways you make your friends and loved ones feel significant? It's just as important to think about how you make other people feel and how you contribute to helping them meet their needs. For example, **you can make someone feel significant by simply letting them know that you're thinking of them or telling them that you love them**. You can buy them a gift, send a birthday message, help them with something. **These are all valid ways to make someone else feel significant** and, crucially, happier — both things that are linked to the hormone and neurotransmitter **SEROTONIN**, which you might have heard of as a **'HAPPY HORMONE'** due to its role in **treatments for mental health issues like depression and anxiety**. It's so easy to make someone feel significant nowadays — **all we have to do is write a message and press send!**

Have a think about where you find significance and if it's misplaced. **The more you start looking at what's behind your actions, the clearer the source of the significance you seek should become.** Are you motivated by respect from others — whether that's among your peers in the classroom or your elders on the street? **Are these people good sources from which to seek significance** — loving family members, those from within your smallest circle back in chapter 2 — or are they simply the popular kids you want to look cool in front of? **Or is it self-respect, something from within, that's driving you?**

Many adults I've worked with still had bad habits and patterns that they formed when they were teenagers. But when you get a smartphone, every year as a minimum you normally must do a system upgrade, right? So why do people think that our own software doesn't need updating? **If the world around us is constantly shifting, if we are constantly experiencing new things and change, how is it that some people think they should stay the same?** We have to change our habits.

To do this, we need to understand the purpose of our actions and **determine whether our habits are moving us closer to who we want to be or further away**. Remember my **future-pacing self** at the start of this book? You want to make sure that your decisions and choices are helping you get closer to the person you want to be — and to the future you set out for yourself at the start of this book. ***Will you always do the right thing? No, no human does. I have made so many mistakes — but we learn from them and move on.***

CHAPTER 4

THE RUSH - CHOOSE YOUR OWN ADVENTURE

I had been threatened in the past with knives. I'd had a couple of near-miss experiences, **but the first time I'd felt a blade against my skin and had blood flow from me was when I was seventeen**.

We had just celebrated my birthday — my family and friends had all come together and we had some food at a nearby restaurant we liked. Afterwards, me and my boys headed into Central London to walk around, have fun and try to buy alcohol. Growing up, I wasn't raised around drink, and from a religious point of view it also wasn't accepted. **But I was at an age where I was curious. I was trying new things and wanted to fit in, and alcohol was one of those things.**

My boys and I jumped on the bus and were sharing a few bottles between us. **We all quickly got tipsy, but because I had never really drunk before I was in a more vulnerable state.** Getting off at Marble Arch, we walked the rest of the way to Trocadero — the hotspot at the time — which had a big arcade, bumper cars and a punch-bag machine. As we approached, we saw some girls standing there looking at us, so we looked back.

We huddled and started planning who was going to ask for their numbers. **I was always a little more confident, and though I had been rejected multiple times before, I had learned not to take it personally.** I could see there was a bunch of younger guys hanging around them, but I wasn't sure if they were together. As I was about to approach one of the girls, a guy came up to me.

BOY: WHAT YOU DOING TRYING TO INTIMIDATE MY YOUNGERS, FAM?

ME: WHAT YOU TALKING ABOUT, BRUV? I'M NOT EVEN LOOKIN' AT DEM.

BOY: MY YOUNGER TOLD ME THAT YOU'VE BEEN EYEING THEM UP, SO WHAT'S GOOD, THOUGH?

ME: ACTUALLY, WE WERE EYEING UP THOSE GYALS, SO MOVE FROM ME, MY YOUT.

BOY: WHAT DID YOU CALL ME?

ME: A YOUT. MOVE FROM ME.

The boy was at least two years younger than me. **He flicked out a knife and, before I knew it, he was holding the tip of it directly inside of my belly**

button. Not only was he holding it there, but he was twisting clockwise, then anticlockwise, while tilting his head and looking into my eyes.

BOY: WHO'S THE YOUT NOW?
ME: YOU MUST BE DUMB TO FINK YOU CAN PULL OUT A KNIFE ON MAN. YOU'RE NOT EVEN FROM THESE ENDS, ARE YOU?
BOY: NAH, G, MAN'S FROM SOUTH INNIT, BUT RIGHT NOW NONE OF THAT MATTERS.
ME: WELL, IT DOES BECAUSE IF I MAKE ONE PHONE CALL, YOU'RE ALL GOING TO GET DEALT WITH.
BOY: I THINK YOU'RE FORGETTING WHAT I CAN DO TO YOU RIGHT NOW. YOU WON'T EVEN BE ABLE TO DRAW FOR YOUR PHONE.

I knew he was right, and though I kept pulling my stomach inward, he kept that blade firmly against me.

ME: SO WHAT YOU SAYING, YOU GOING TO USE DAT TING?

He pulled his knife away and told me that I was lucky as he started laughing and walked back to his friends. **My boys kept asking me if I was OK, and I wasn't.** I leaned against a post. I ran scenarios through my head about what to do, and then I remembered that, for some reason, in my back pocket I had a butter knife I'd stolen from the restaurant. **All I kept focusing on was him telling me I was lucky and how he laughed at me.** I started crying. This was a normal thing for me. **When I got really angry, I would start crying.** Not your usual cry when you're making noises, just tears rolling down my cheeks. **My boys knew I was going to do something.**

Unbeknown to me, my friend had called my brothers-in-law to come and help out. I stood up from where I was, pulled out the butter knife from my back pocket and ran towards Leicester Square looking for that boy. **I pushed anyone who was in my way, searching for him like a predator looking for its prey.**

A bit like my brother, when I saw red, there was no stopping me. In that moment, my brothers-in -law pulled up and jumped out. **They could see I was in a state and that I would do something very stupid**, so we all jumped in the car and went home. **It was definitely the right decision**, and it's another moment I think back on that could have ended very differently.

HUSTLING AGAIN

I only stayed in college for a few months before I quit. **There was a part of me that didn't feel I was smart enough to go to university**, so I questioned why I was even going to college. **But I also felt directionless. Just before enrolling, another friend of mine was stabbed and killed, right around the corner from where I lived.** It was hard for everyone to process. **Our friends and families were broken-hearted and angry, and I was scared.**

People were getting stabbed way too often now, and not just in postcode wars, which is when it's one area against another. You could get killed by people in your own area for getting into altercations. **Our areas were supposed to be where we could feel safe, but that wasn't the case anymore.** In my college, there were very few people I knew who were from my area. So what did this mean? I was slipping. I had a few run-ins with some guys, and **I questioned whether it was worth putting my life at risk to travel to a college.** My friend had just died.

KIDS WERE NOW NOT ONLY CARRYING KNIVES — THEY HAD MACHETES AND ZOMBIE KNIVES. SO I LEFT, BUT I HAD NO PLAN, NO OTHER COLLEGE TO GO TO.

Though my parents made things work without going to uni, I had already been denied over fifty jobs from applications I made, **probably because employers were judging me based on appearance**, and it made me believe that I wasn't good enough or smart enough to get a normal job. **I had no money and no direction, and it felt horrible.**

I knew I had to start hustling again, but I didn't think I wanted to go back to drugs. I mean, I was almost sure I didn't want to get back into drugs — **it seemed like all the deaths I heard about at that time were connected to drugs and gangs**.

I worked in some markets and made some cash-in-hand money, **but it wasn't enough**. Finally, it felt like I caught a break. I heard about a woman in Camden Market who was getting in replicas of handbags, designer belts and even watches. I asked another friend of mine to make an introduction and he did. **She was your typical backstreet hustler, and I liked her.** I wasn't an expert on designer goods, so I took pictures of everything, picked up a couple of samples and went to compare them to the real things in Selfridges. I was impressed.

I started off buying and selling the belts. Gucci and Louis Vuitton, mostly. I sold these to friends who were on my course, to family friends and people from the area. Soon I was pulling a suitcase full of handbags and belts as well as carrying black bin bags full of products around Central London. **Why? Because I had already sold to everyone I knew and now I wanted to sell to people with money** who wanted to look rich on a budget. So I targeted the banks. It got to the point where I would turn up after banking hours; they opened the doors for me and they went crazy. **There were four banks on this high street, all of whom were buying from me and telling their friends about me.**

One of the bank managers, who became one of my best customers, sat me down and asked, 'What are you going to do with the money?' I said, **'It's not a crazy amount of money, but I will buy new stock and keep hustling.'** She said that I should put some into a bank account and save it. She helped me open up a platinum account at the bank, which was usually for big businesspeople, but she was the manager. **She taught me how to use it and she then introduced me to other bank managers she knew.**

I had managed to impress even myself with my level of resourcefulness. People think that everyone who gets involved with drugs does it because they love it. Yes, some do, but others like me, **who weren't given a chance in society, had no other choice**. I tried doing what I could to avoid that life, but it was hard and tiring.

Around the same time, some guys I knew from the gym said they could get me some easy work. I sat and looked at two black bin bags I had in my room, full of T-shirts ready to be sold, **and I realised I was so lonely. I had very little interaction with other guys my age, and I was craving that again**.
I was scared to my core about getting involved with other gangs in other areas, **but at the same time this could solve my loneliness problem** and give me more road experience.

BAD BUSINESS

I decided to meet the people offering this easy work. I jumped on the Victoria line, got out from the underground station and a car pulled up. I was told to jump in, **and they put a hood over my head**. I thought calmly to myself, *OK, I am dying today.*

The car stopped. We all got out. I was walked into a building. **I could only see the floor from the opening at the bottom of the hood.** They took the hood off me, and one of my guys was there along with other guys who were much older. My guy said, 'You wanted in – this is your chance, fam.' They sat me down and asked me questions, and I could only assume they were trying to work me out. **At this point I was questioning why I liked to put myself into situations I didn't know I would get out of!** I then had to have a chat alone with the main guy. I told him everything as honestly as possible, and he said the same thing to me as the previous older I'd worked for: that I was smarter than most youngers he comes across.

He asked me questions using as few words as possible. I didn't know whether to look directly in his eyes to show that I had no fear (even though I did) or to avoid looking in his eyes as a sign of respect (but that could also have made me look weak). He didn't smile, and it was almost as if he didn't blink either. There's a certain look that some people have when you know they have been through madness and have stories to tell, and he had those eyes.

He told me that the only reason I was there was because my guy had vouched for me and told him that I was a fast runner and could handle myself if anything went to arms. Then he said that before I did any work for him, **I had to prove myself**. He made a certain noise with his mouth, and everyone got up. They all understood what it meant — but I didn't. We all got into two separate cars. **Some of the guys wore gloves, and everyone had masks on.**

We drove around for at least forty-five minutes looking for someone. **I was told when we found him that we were going to jump him and put him in the back of the car. I was terrified.** All I kept saying in my head was, *I'm going to prison, I'm going to prison.* But in the very back of my mind, I was a little excited too. My life was boring at this time: I sold fake goods, I was single, I wasn't part of any clubs or sports team. I would spend most of my evenings alone watching movies. **Being with these guys in the car was the most exciting thing that had happened to me for a long time.**

But it didn't take long for me to realise that the road wasn't a joke. **These guys were committed. The way they moved and spoke about it was as if it was a piece of land they had bought and somebody was trespassing.** Suddenly it crossed my mind that they might not be looking for some guy. **They might be planning to do something to me.**

I was sat in the middle at the back of the car. I don't think I said one word during this whole period. The car had tinted windows, so I couldn't really see outside properly, which made me feel a little claustrophobic. **The guy driving seemed the scariest. He didn't say much; he had multiple scars and kept looking at me in the mirror with a menacing stare.** The guy next to him was the shortest but seemed to be the most excited. He kept saying, 'Watch when we find you, you think you're bad, yeah.' He was smoking a spliff, which kept blowing directly into my face. But none of them seem scared we might be stopped by the police. **THEY WERE INVINCIBLE.**

Suddenly, one of the guys shouted, 'YO, YO, I SEE HIM!' They slowed the car down, **and I was told to**

jump out with another guy and beat him up. I froze. I kept thinking I couldn't fight unless I was angry. But I also knew that if I was going to get in with these guys, then I had to prove myself. **I couldn't be soft; I had to make the right impression.** I didn't know who this guy was or what he had done; I just knew I had to hurt him. **We jumped out and kept landing shots until two of the bigger guys came, carried him to the back of the car park and then put him in the back of one of the cars.**

One side of me was questioning what the hell I was doing here; the other was saying this was what I needed to experience. The cars drove for a while, then stopped again. This time we all got out. **They dragged the guy out from the back, gave me a black latex glove to put on and put a Rambo knife in my hand.**

They filmed the guy and tried to humiliate him. **It was hard for me to watch any of this, but to them it was all entertainment.** The older told me that I had to **hold the knife to his face** and ask him if he was ever going to shot weed in the ends again.

Now I understood what he had done wrong. He had been selling on someone else's turf. **On road, you don't shot in someone else's postcode or on their block.** It was time to put all of my rehearsals to the test. I tried to make my voice deeper. I had half of my face covered, and I approached the guy. If I had been alone, I knew I wouldn't have been able to do this, but these guys gassed me up and somehow I felt I was able to. I stared into his eyes and did exactly as I was asked. **I put the blade on his cheek bone and asked him if he was ever going to shot in these ends again.** He said no. I looked at the older and he shook his head.

I pressed the knife more firmly against his face and this time, in a much louder tone, asked him if he was going to shot in these ends again. These weren't even my ends that I was defending, but I had to act like I was part of the gang. I had tears in my eyes, and the guy was crying. He had snot dripping down on to his chest and was looking at me, begging me not to do anything.

I felt sick, but I also realised that I had now become like that younger boy who put a knife in my belly button. **I thought it might feel good to hold power in my hands**, to have guys behind me who were on it. But none of those rehearsals prepared me for any of this, **to see a man so humiliated, to hear the sound of his beard scrape against the blade I held against his skin**.

I was pulled back and told to head inside. **I couldn't stop thinking about how humiliated he had been.** And, although it was messed up, I felt cool being around these guys. The older spudded me (gave me a fist bump) and told me he couldn't have me on road yet, but I could help him bag his drugs. **I had a huge smile on my face because it was something I had done before and I felt confident doing it.**

The work with him wasn't always there, so I was still selling the designer replicas, and I also joined a company my dad was working with. I had no singular focus — I enjoyed having a few streams of income and was constantly thinking about what else I could do. **I knew that I didn't want to be doing what I was doing with that gang for a long time.** I wanted to know that I could walk away if I chose to, **but my involvement with them gave me a thrill that my other stuff never did**.

Sometimes, I would meet up with them and we would just go out to move to people, which meant robbing them for their money, phones or anything they had. **Some of those guys had zero fear.** It was almost as if they lived off that type of lifestyle. **But all that excitement soon wore off when I was robbed myself . . .**

THE TURNING POINT

I was at a bus stop and had two big bags on me — one was full of True Religion jeans, which had now become the new hot-selling product, and the other one had bags and watches that I was selling. **I was approached by one guy at the bus stop who asked me where I got my jeans from. I told him that I sold them.** He said that his family were over today and they would 100 buy stuff from me. **We agreed to meet nearby at a certain time and he would help me sell some stuff.**

I felt optimistic about making some sales, so we met and I followed the guy through an alleyway, **at which point two guys jumped out, hit me on the head and kept beating me**. I dropped one bag and tried to throw a shot back, but I felt horrible from the blow to the head. **I was now on the ground, curled up in a ball, taking the kicks and stomps** while holding on to the bag full of watches. These were the most expensive items I had.

One of the guys **stepped on my face** and forced the bag from my hands, and I watched as they took off. I got up, gathered what was left of my stuff and started going after the guy with the watches. **I was hurt pretty bad but I was still a fast runner and could follow where he went** and which corners he took. Finally, I saw him standing at the bottom of a block of flats. **By the time I got to him, he had already gone inside**, but as I approached the door, I saw the flat number he had buzzed flash on the monitor twice before going blank.

I waited until someone left the flat block so that I could go inside. I found the flat he had called and I knocked on the door. I heard a bunch of whispering, and a girl opened it. I asked her if anyone else was here. She said only her and her sick grandma. **I told her I'd just got robbed and I was pretty sure that the guy rang this number. She pretended she didn't know what I was talking about.**

I had a feeling she was lying, but I also didn't know who else was in there. I made my way back outside, and right at that moment I got a call from one of my olders. His first question was, 'Where are you?', almost like he knew something had just happened to me. I told him I'd just got moved to. He said, 'Wait there and give me ten minutes.'

I CAN'T LIE, I FELT HORRIBLE. I HAD BEEN TRICKED AND FELT LIKE A FOOL – BUT THAT IS WHAT LIFE WAS LIKE ON ROAD. Two cars soon pulled up. My older had called up some local guys and they looked serious. The main guy asked me what door number it was. I told him, and he ran over to the flat block.

He put one leg up and pulled the ground floor door hard, and it opened. We all went upstairs; he told me to knock on the door again and try to look inside the flat. **The rest of the guys were standing and crouching on either side of the door.**

I knocked, and the girl came back wearing a towel and blocking the entrance. I couldn't see inside.

I asked her if she was sure she didn't see anyone run up here, and she promised me she hadn't. At that moment, she went to adjust her towel and I saw for a split second that she was wearing one of my watches. I knew she was lying and I was pissed.

As soon as she closed the door, **the guys got up, got their tools out and booted the door in**. They ran in quick to make sure no one had time to draw any weapons. **All three guys who'd jumped me were there**, and, as you probably guessed, there was no grandma.

There was a huge fight. I grabbed the girl's arm, took my watch from her wrist and went to chat to the main guy who'd robbed me. He was in the bathroom and one of the guys who was with me asked him why he'd robbed me. **He said I was an easy target and he thought I wasn't from the ends.** The guy punched him and he fell back into the bathtub, where the water was still running.

He got back up. I felt embarrassed by what he'd said, so I punched him back down.

At this point, someone slipped a knife into my hand and I started pointing it at him. I had held a knife to someone before, **but I had never stabbed anyone and I wasn't sure if I wanted to**. The guy was standing there, shaking and repeatedly apologising to me. He said, 'I swear I didn't know you were from the ends – I haven't seen you before.'

As I mentioned earlier, people create divisions over anything. If you lived in the same area but were from a different school, that was enough reason to have beef with each other. If you wanted to visit a new area and were caught slipping, one of the first questions you'd get asked was, 'What ends are you from?' And if you were from an area which was known to have beef with theirs, something was about to go down.

At that moment, I felt strong. I had a guy older than me begging me for mercy. Then another elder walked in, saw me holding the knife against him, took it off me and said, 'That's not happening.'

I was so happy he did that. As we left, the girl was crying and the other guys were on the floor. They looked hurt. I grabbed my watches and we walked off. **I was scared and buzzing with adrenaline, but above all, I was just glad no one got stabbed and that I had my watches back.**

DANCE WITH THE UNKNOWN

At the start of the book I explained that sometimes we have **BREAKTHROUGH MOMENTS** – where a significant shift occurs that has the power to change your future. **This was one of them. It was at this point I knew I had to stop carrying knives.** I didn't think I could ever be capable of stabbing someone, but the whole experience made me question that. It scared me. **There were times when I wished I still had one on me, like when I was robbed again.** But I didn't want to be one stupid mistake away from potentially ending someone's life and ruining mine.

There was even a time when I became obsessed with knives and swords. At one point it wasn't just about carrying a knife; it was about how big and scary the knife was. **People still carry machetes and swords for this reason. But the damage they can cause is irreversible.**

Most young people I knew, including myself, carried knives because we were **genuinely scared of what could happen to us** on road and sometimes even in school. Although this seems like an obvious thing to do, it really should not be. **I'd much prefer young people learned to run and call for help rather than stand there in a knife fight hoping they win.** If you won, that would mean you had seriously injured someone or even killed them. **Nobody actually wins!** The knife you chose to carry for protection is now the key piece of evidence in a **MURDER**, and **multiple lives have been ruined**.

I remember a time in school when one guy in the year below me decided to carry a knife because he thought he was an easy target. A fight broke out, and one of the guys fighting knew this kid had a knife on him, so he took it off him then **STABBED** the guy he was fighting. So now a knife one guy carried for protection was being used by another guy in a fight to stab someone. **Use knives to cut bread, vegetables or fruit, not as weapons. Keep them at home.**

I remember being my younger self; I remember the thoughts I had and what I got up to. **But now I can look back and understand why I really did what I did.** Getting into fights, being chased by the police, becoming involved with the wrong type of people – **I did a lot of it because I was bored.** These activities broke up the mundane routine of the day and gave me something all humans need – the feeling of uncertainty because I never knew what would happen and **that made me feel a rush of excitement,** and the feeling of variety because it made things interesting. **My friends and I were addicted to the adrenaline – the rush of it all.**

DOSAGE: Adrenaline

ADRENALINE is a hormone that is released when we're **SCARED OR STRESSED**. It puts us into a **fight-or-flight state** and, you probably guessed right, **ADRENALINE** is also the **neurotransmitter attached to our need for uncertainty and variety**.

People do all sorts of things for uncertainty and variety. They jump out of planes, swim with sharks, get involved with gangs, cheat on their partners, go on holidays, take part in competitions, get piercings and much more. But on a more basic level, we do things every day that give us variety - such as wearing different clothes during the week, not eating the same food every day, walking a different way home, watching a new TV show or taking on a new hobby.

I shared with you how, back then, I had different ways of making money. **I needed the variety.** I got involved with certain things to give me new experiences and emotions that I wasn't getting in my day-to-day life. **Humans don't like to feel bored – we need new stimuli, new things to get us excited, and we need change.**

Ever wonder why sometimes the things that are bad feel so good? That's adrenaline. And it's what gangs live off. If you're in a gang, every moment of the day is fuelled with adrenaline because you are around things that pose risk, that are often illegal and that are usually rewarded with money, loyalty or the feeling of respect.

I know this may not be a reality for you . . . or perhaps it is. Maybe there's someone you know who is getting involved in some questionable activity and won't walk away. **Speaking from experience, when we're growing up, we think we know it all but we don't.** We are easily influenced, and half the time we don't know why we do what we do, and for some, this ends in very bad situations.

A lot of people hardly leave their local area and some don't believe that there would be anything out there for them if they did. **This can make their dreams smaller**, and the idea of being the next top kid in their ends or having respect becomes their ambition. **This is where gangs find their power** — they offer the promise of achieving these small ambitions, **of feeling important and seen**. But it's a slippery slope to some very dark places. As you can see from my story, **grooming is a process.** Young people get chosen and convinced to start taking on small jobs which later lead to bigger and more dangerous things. **If this is happening to you, or you know someone who is experiencing it, there are resources at the back of this book and I would recommend that you get a responsible adult involved.** If it's a friend you're trying to help, they may not want you getting involved, but by doing so **you could potentially be saving their life**. If it's you who is trying to get out, then you will need to be **BRAVE** and let your parents or a trusted adult know what you have been up to, **how it is making you feel and that you need their help**.

Gangs are an extreme example. But all of us, no matter who we are, seek rushes of adrenaline in different ways. It could be playing up in school, sneaking out at night, speeding on a bike or doing something your parents said not to. **These actions can feel exciting and offer a temporary thrill or rush, but they can lead to trouble.**

Adrenaline isn't a bad thing in itself. It's how we choose to experience it. So how can you fulfil your need for variety, for thrills and excitement, without going down the wrong track? Try sport. I had track and field, but it can be anything. You could also start a side hustle, learn a new skill, find something you can get competitive about such as taking part in chess competitions, perform in a dance group or learn a martial art. If it doesn't challenge you, it will never change you. **You can use adrenaline to work for you by setting yourself challenges.** Think about what excites you and make POSITIVE CHOICES that help you have a more **fulfilling and trouble-free life**. I already mentioned how easy it is to be influenced, and if it's someone who you look up to or respect, **they can easily convince you to take an interest in something you normally wouldn't**. But take a moment and step back. *Question why you are doing what you are doing.*

I've sat down with many adults who said they wished they'd made better choices in their teens, because sometimes the choices you make in your teens can affect you for the rest of your life. So why not start getting things right? **Invest in your future self through the choices you make now.**

At the start of the book, I asked who you want to BE and how you could get there. **Think about it:**

What are your habits when you are bored and alone? Are these things you can talk about and be proud of, or are they things you would be embarrassed about? What habits do you and your friends have when you are all together and bored?

After a certain amount of repetition, the mind and the body want to experience something different. People also get bored of relationships, careers and even hobbies. **So it's important to try new things, to bring variety into your life and mix things up.**

CHANGE IS GOOD

In school we get taught how to expand our knowledge in certain subjects, **but not how to change our mindset or strengthen it**. No one ever spoke to me about identity, limiting beliefs or perspective.

I remember years ago, when I bumped into friends I hadn't seen for a long time, **one of the first things they said to me was that I had changed**. They said this as if it was a bad thing. But for me, I wouldn't want to stay the same. **I want to develop.**

Some people are unaware of what should change or that they have the ability to change in the first place. I am here to tell you:

YOU HAVE THE ABILITY TO CHANGE YOURSELF, MAKE DECISIONS AND INFLUENCE YOUR OWN FUTURE.

NO ONE IS PERFECT. We all make bad decisions. But if there is something you've been doing that's given you a rush, and you now realise it's bad for you and you want to stop, **try replacing it with something more positive that will send you in the right direction**.

Remember, earlier I said it's not about what we are doing; it's about how that thing makes us feel. **We are all chasing feelings: we want more pleasure and excitement and less pain and suffering.**

CHAPTER 5

SECURITY - RINSE AND REPEAT

Something I noticed about myself when I was younger was that anytime I got involved in a fight or hit someone, **I felt bad about it later**. There were some days when I would even cry in bed because of the pain the other person must have felt, **and I just felt sad overall because I really hated conflict**. It took me a long time to calm down after becoming angry, **and I have had so many wasted moments because I was angry and not able to take things in**.

It got to a point where I had to admit to myself that I wasn't like some other people out there, **and that was OK. I didn't need to measure myself up to be like anyone else.** At this point in my life, I was helping my dad with his business to market and sell health products. One day I was sitting on the Victoria line heading into Central London to a conference run by the big American company who supplied us with the products. I picked up the newspaper on the seat in front of me and what I saw really bothered me. **Across the pages were pictures of brown-skinned boys who had either been killed or were going to jail.**

I really needed to pull away from the guys in South London, because I wasn't just cutting and bagging anymore; I was now making deliveries for them.

The thrill of that lifestyle no longer excited me, and nor did I feel I needed it. **I knew I didn't want my face appearing in the newspaper for any of the same reasons as those other boys.** I had to figure out how to get out. *I was so worried about my future.* There were so many examples and omens pointing to why I needed to start making better decisions and get away from the road life – I JUST HAD TO START DOING IT. I was also worried about getting out but then falling back into the same cycle of needing that exposure again. **I had to find a healthier, safer alternative.**

I got to the conference a little late, but as I walked in, **people were dancing and jumping**, and I thought I'd walked into the wrong room. **I'd never seen that type of energy before, but I liked it.** There was a guest speaker there who talked about his life story, about **how where you came from didn't need to be where you ended up and how we can change**

if we put in the work. I was so focused on every word he said because **I needed to hear it**. The company started recognising and awarding people on stage who were doing well in the business. **I knew I wanted to be on that stage.** I found a new motivation, a new goal to work towards. On the lunch break, one of the attendees told me that the speaker was paid $10,000 for his talk. It had been no longer than an hour!

I KNEW I HAD TO TALK TO THIS GUY. People were queuing up to take pictures with him. I waited patiently. It got to my turn, and he asked in his strong American accent, 'You want a picture, son?' I replied, 'Actually I don't. I mean, I do, but there's something else.' He looked a little taken aback. I asked if I could speak to him in private, and he promised we could at the end.

The end of the day finally came. He called me over and I started telling him about the kinds of things I was doing. **I told him about selling the products on the street, about getting involved in a gang to make some money.** I told him that watching him speak on stage gave me an idea for something I would like to do, **as I would like to inspire people**

too. He put his hand on my shoulder, looked me straight in the eye and said, 'Son, if you don't change the people you're hanging around with or change the things that you're doing, you may not live long enough to do what I'm doing.'

Those words rang in my ear as if he was saying it on repeat. He gave me a hug and I made my way home. The words he shared helped me make my mind up, and I knew I no longer wanted anything to do with the road life. It was a real **BREAKTHROUGH MOMENT** for me. The thing is, I had known this for such a long time but I really didn't know what else was out there for me.

I had multiple confirmations as to why I wanted nothing to do with it. I got robbed badly, I could have stabbed someone and now I was being told by someone I really looked up to that if I didn't choose wisely, I could die young.

Thinking of dying scared me, and thinking of dying without having truly lived terrified me.

There's nothing I wanted more than to change my circumstances and this left me with the question, **HOW DOES SOMEONE CHANGE?** I knew I had to make different choices, but I also had to make a mental shift; this was something I heard the motivational speaker mention in his talk but I just didn't know where to start. **I decided to start learning again, to become a student of wisdom and personal development.**

It was at this point in my life that I really started to get into reading books. I never really read books growing up. Some of my friends had read the *Harry Potter* books, but I had no interest in them. **My father had some personal development books**, which I would take from his shelves and read one by one, and with the money I had I would buy myself books on similar topics because **I was interested in the idea of self-change, self-empowerment and identity**.

Although to other teenagers these books may have been boring, for me, they were the most exciting things I could read. I started learning about psychology. I started reading about neurolinguistic programming and understanding how the words we use, the way we think, all of these things combined, change the actions that we take and form our mindset around different thoughts and beliefs.

There was one night when I had to make another delivery for the gang, and as the older was preparing the bag, I asked him a question that surprised him. **I asked him why he never got out of this lifestyle.** He looked at me and said there was no getting out; this was my life now. When I said to him, 'Yeah, but you can always start again – you can always find something new to do,' he got angry with me.

I apologised and told him I wanted to talk to him as I didn't want to work for him anymore and do these types of jobs. He smiled and said, 'Fam, you're in now, that's just the way it is.' **I told him surely there was a way for me to get out** – I wasn't on road in the same way other youngsters were. I'd only been bagging up drugs. **This couldn't be my life forever, could it?** He looked at me but didn't say anything. As I got ready to leave, one of the other guys came up to me, grabbed my jumper and said, 'Bruv, are you dumb? What's all this talk about you leaving? You asked me to get you in, now you're in, fam.'

I told him I was grateful that he got me in, but from the very beginning, I hadn't wanted to get too involved. **He looked at me pityingly** and said, 'Nah, fam, it doesn't work like that.' I said, 'Yeah, well, it will have to work like that because I can't keep doing what I'm doing.'

He didn't like that. I left the place and made my usual route to the drop-off point, and for some reason this time something felt weird **(ALWAYS TRUST YOUR GUT)**. I made sure nobody was following me — I ran down some roads just to make sure I was ahead of anyone if they were following me and I took certain back streets to avoid high roads. Then as I turned down one alleyway, I heard the words:

'THERE HE IS.'
I HAD BEEN SET UP.

There were four guys in front of me. Two of them were on BMXs, and I thought there was no point in me trying to be a hero, so I quickly turned back the other way and ran, but then more guys appeared. Whenever I got into stressful situations, I always tried to slow down my breathing, and somehow everything around me also slowed down because I was trying to calculate my options, playing different scenarios in my head.

A skinny guy on a BMX said, 'Yo, fam, throw over the bag.' Someone had told them I was coming. **There were only a few people who knew that route – it was definitely a set-up.** He hissed, 'Fam, you're not walking out of here until I have that bag.' **I tried to be brave.** I told him that we had a problem, then. I don't know why I was trying to be Superman, because the odds were **at least one of them had a knife on him**, and even if we got into a fight, I wasn't going to take down seven guys by myself. So I thought, *OK, I can't fight them, but maybe I can outrun them.*

I took the bag off my back slowly, just to give myself time to plan something. I held both of the straps firmly in my grip. I was looking at all of their feet, **what was in their hands**. I walked towards the guy on the BMX, and as I approached him, **I figured the only way I could escape was to barge through the gap between the two guys on the left**. As I got closer, I looked to the ground, then suddenly I pretended to throw the bag at him, which made him flinch. **I had half a second to push through those guys, and I did, still holding on to the bag.**

I ran down the alleyway as if my life depended on it. **Which maybe it did. But then I slipped.** Everything went in slow motion. I could see them getting closer. **I was scrambling to my knees. And I made a quick change of plan.** Instead of going out towards the main road, I jumped a brick wall to my left, not knowing what was there. **I got over the wall, threw the bag on to my back and kept running.** I was near a park and kept looking for crowds of people to get lost in. **But there was no one around.**

Running with one eye over my shoulder, I could see the BMX racing towards me, the handlebars flinging from side to side with the speed. **Soon the rest of the guys were behind him.** I hopped another fence, tore my jeans in the process, and ran down what I thought would be an alleyway into a block of flats. **BUT IT WAS A DEAD END.**

I turned back as quickly as possible to try and get out of this spot, but it was too late. **They had caught up with me and now my odds of escaping were even more slim.** One of the guys said, 'You know what, fam, we were just going to take the bag from you, but because you made me run, you're going to get it.' I didn't quite know what my options were, **but I feared for my life**. So I handed the bag over and that was it. The first guy landed his shot, then the second guy landed his, and there was no point even trying to fight back. I firmed the shots, **stood for as long as I could, then dropped to the floor and curled up into a ball, waiting for the moment when it would be over**.

As they were kicking me and stepping on me, I thought, **AT WHAT MOMENT WILL I GET STABBED?** Then I heard something that confused me. There was a guy I'd hung out with in college who would always say the word 'BOOM' every time he landed a hit. And now, every time I was getting kicked by a guy in a balaclava, he was saying 'BOOM' too. The final blow landed and I had to let him know that I knew it was him. **He was the one walking away holding the bag.** I shouted out his name, which made him stop. He still had his balaclava on and as he looked back at me, I smiled and said the word 'BOOM' back to him.

A MATTER OF LIFE OR DEATH

As soon as they left, I got a call from the older asking me if I had made the drop. **The timing was too synced for it to be random**, but I pretended that he didn't know, so I told him **I had just been robbed. HE WENT MAD.**

I had to think fast and be smart. I told him I was somewhere else and quickly ran to get there before him, **because I knew there was a spot I could watch from without him seeing me**. I sprinted as fast as I could but I was in pain — my left hamstring had been kicked real bad and was almost contracting every time I used my left leg. I got to the spot, put my phone on silent and waited for him to turn up. **Someone turned up, but it wasn't him.** I remembered exactly who this guy was because he had on the same hat, the same black gloves: he was the one who drove the car when I had to go and jump that guy to prove myself when I first got introduced. **This guy didn't talk much and he had a nickname, DUPPY — which meant to KILL or, in some cultures, GHOST.**

This guy wasn't there to give me a lift, and now I knew what they meant by **once you're in, you're in**. **THESE GUYS WEREN'T LETTING ME GO.** He pulled out his phone, made a call and then the older phoned me back. **I was trying to think of what to say if I answered the phone, but I couldn't think of anything, so I turned the phone off**, took out the SIM card, snapped it and dropped each part in a different bin or drain hole.

I knew I had to get myself out of this area as soon as I could, **because if I didn't, I had no idea what would happen to me, but it wouldn't be anything good**. I didn't want to stand and wait at a bus stop because they would know which buses went in my direction, so instead I ran in the opposite direction to catch a train one stop earlier. **MY BODY FELT BUSTED AND MY HEART WAS RACING, BUT I KNEW THIS RUN WAS A MATTER OF LIFE OR DEATH.**

The twelve-minute run felt like it was thirty minutes, **because I feared that any group I ran past or any car that drove past me would be them**. I had an Oyster card with money on it, but for the sake of time, I jumped over the barriers and ran down to the platform as fast as I could. I got on that tube, found a carriage that had as many people as possible and sat down, **praying to get home**. As we approached where I would normally get on to go back home, **I had a crazy amount of anxiety, fearing they would be there checking each carriage, looking for me**. But then the doors closed, the train was on its way and **I felt like I had just escaped an early death. I started to cry**.

MAKING A STEP IN THE RIGHT DIRECTION

Once I got home, I got changed and started praying straight away. **I kept my head on the prayer mat, thanking God repeatedly because I knew the situation could have become much worse.** I kept thinking about the words the motivational speaker had shared with me and knew I was making a step in the right direction. **I kept up my spiritual practice, I kept on reading and I created a routine for myself which included going to the gym and developing my side hustle.** I say 'side hustle' because I was too young to be officially part of the company, but by helping my dad, I was able to gain experience and learn the ropes, and I was put in charge of presentation skills and delivering training to new staff.

Every day, usually with my dad or sometimes alone, I would go out to busy high streets to try and recruit people. I gave short, snappy street-side presentations and invited them to our weekly presentations in the hope that they would like what they saw and sign up to our team to recruit new team members and ultimately make more sales. People did come and many people did sign up. **This was the first time I wasn't living a double life.** I didn't have to sneak off anywhere or go do random jobs, **AND I WAS LOVING IT**. I met like-minded people and I started to see the power of consistency.

In the beginning, there were times when I missed the excitement of the road life, because it had become part of an identity that I'd built. But I had seen enough to know that I wanted nothing to do with it. I wasn't going to be part of the stereotype. I wasn't born to die for a postcode or a block of flats.

WHO MADE UP THESE RULES ANYWAY?

I graduated from an IT course I enrolled on to and I had an interview with Microsoft coming up. Meanwhile, the company I had been working with were closing down, and now I had boxes of health drinks piled up in my bedroom, hundreds of bottles. Each bottle could easily sell for £25, and I realised I had grands just sitting there. **It was time to put my hustler hat back on and to start working the streets AGAIN. But this time I was going to do it differently.** I approached health shops, salons, barber shops, gyms and legit companies. People were buying — **the only issue was these bottles were heavy and I was getting tired of lugging them around.**

So I thought differently. I decided to only sell to people and shops who wanted large numbers to sell and make a profit with. **Within a month I had two gyms stocking my drinks, as well as one Caribbean restaurant, a Colombian boutique shop and two salons.** This was an amazing feeling. I had a little black book where I kept a log of all the inventory, and once a week on a Friday I would cycle round to collect payment and drop off more stock. **THIS WAS THE LIFE!**

It had been a long time since I'd felt secure and balanced. When I was doing those odd jobs on road, sure, I had some money coming in, **but there was so much anxiety and stress that came with it**. When I was selling the bags, belts and watches, it was fun and exciting, but when I thought about what I was actually selling, I didn't feel proud of myself and the profit margins on those products weren't huge. **In my experience, it's much better to earn less in a safe and legal way over a long period of time than to earn more in a risky, illegal way in a short period of time.**

I now didn't have to look over my shoulder or feel the need to prove myself to anyone. I was working on myself and trying to make better life choices, which would help me break through so many limiting beliefs and patterns I had created and been stuck with.

FEARS FOR THE FUTURE

Things were going well, but I spent a lot of time by myself. **Probably too much time. I saw my boys every now and then, but I wasn't in the best mental space.** I didn't know what was wrong with me or why I felt the way I felt, **but on reflection, I was lonely**.

I knew that one day, those bottles sitting in my room would come to an end, and things would change. **I was also living with my brother and we weren't seeing eye to eye on many things.** We were two guys trying to figure out our futures, **and instead of being there for each other, we were at each other's necks.** We argued, we fought. We were both very talented, but we hadn't had the chance to start a promising or safe career. **We had to make ends meet, and that's a stressful way to live.**

I had the interview with Microsoft and they turned me down. This upset me. **I really wanted that job so I could work with people, stop feeling lonely,**

stop living on the edge and have a reliable source of income. To make matters worse, my brother and I had just had a huge fight, which ended in him storming out of the flat. **Shortly after, there was a knock at the door.**

I quietly approached the front door to look through the keyhole. A girl was standing there. I'd never seen her before, so I went into the kitchen and peeped through the curtain to see who else was there.

THANK GOD I DID. THERE WERE FOUR OR FIVE GUYS CROUCHING DOWN BESIDE THE DOOR AND BENEATH THE KITCHEN WINDOW. ONE HAD A BAT, ONE A BATON AND WHEN I SAW THE MACHETE, I KNEW THESE GUYS WERE ON SMOKE (THEY WANTED TO DO DAMAGE).

I also knew that they could boot down the front door if they wanted to, so I quickly crept upstairs and I told myself I had two minutes to pack my stuff and **get the hell out of there**. Based on how old they looked, I knew they were there for me. **But I didn't know why, and I didn't have time to figure this out now.** I stopped, took a deep breath and kept repeating one word: essentials. I grabbed my passport, laptop, inventory book, chargers, clothes and anything else I could.

I never thought I would ever be put in a position where I had to run away from home, but here I was.

They kept banging the door and now a guy was calling my name, saying, 'We know you're in there.' I didn't recognise his voice, which bothered me. I scanned my room one last time, looking for anything else I needed to take, and that was it. **I pushed open my bedroom window, jumped on to the scaffolding that was outside, climbed down into the garden and started running.** I didn't look back. Only once I'd got away would I try to figure out who they were. I ran until I got to the mosque. **I sat in the garden and cried with my head in my hands.**

I FELT LIKE GIVING UP. I had no real social life, no job, potentially no business, no security and now no home. **I thought about the times I had gone out to apply for jobs in person and nobody would give me a chance.** I still felt like I wasn't good enough, even though **I knew deep down that I was a very**

talented young man. I never slept another night in that flat.

That night, I sat in a gazebo in the garden of the mosque where I'd spent a lot of my childhood. It was named after my family's spiritual teacher, and this building was gifted to him by one of his students, the Sultan of Brunei. I had come to this mosque at least twice a month since I was a child, **and just sitting there made me think about Sheikh Nazim, who people travelled all over the world to visit and learn from**. When he walked through this garden, he would spend time looking at the roses, smelling them. **He was present and he paid attention to even the small things.** The way he looked at the world made me think he could see things that I couldn't because of how connected he was. **He always said that everything happens by divine reason, and I started to reflect on that.**

To become a Sufi was to become totally submitted, to chisel away your bad characteristics, bad habits, and essentially empty your cup in order to receive something new, to be open.

I was initially sad and angry that I was going through so much pain, that I had lost so much, but spiritually, I thought, *This is all happening for me, not to me.* Although I got up to no good, I still had spiritual and religious practices that I'd kept throughout my life. **These practices were my foundations.**

There had to be pain involved for me to learn my lesson. If getting out of the gang was too easy then I'd know I could do it again if I ever drifted back into that life – but because it was hard, I knew I couldn't let myself drift back. Because of everything that had happened to me, I felt like God was cutting people off around me and that he wanted me at that mosque. **I thought I had lost everything, but I found myself once again.**

STAND TALL ON STRONG ROOTS

In the last chapter, we looked at the importance of variety. **But we also need the direct opposite of that too — SECURITY, to feel safe and certain.** Why is certainty important? Doesn't it feel nice to know that we can go to sleep with a roof over our heads? That there is something to eat in the morning? But, of course, when there's too much certainty, too much routine, too much familiarity, **guess what you start searching for? *ADRENALINE, variety, new stimuli*** — and I've already shared the dangers the pursuit of too much variety can cause us. **Balance is always important.**

I knew I wanted to get out of gang life, but there was one main thing I was trying to build so that I could make that happen: **A STEADY INCOME.** I needed money to eat and to survive, but most importantly **I needed a steady source of income so that the temptations of the road life would never grip me again.** That's why I went into hustle mode.

I was desperate to get away from the things I used to do.

When I left my house, I wanted to know I didn't have to be alone, that I wasn't a loser and that I could support myself. But we all seek CERTAINTY and SECURITY in different ways. For example, something as simple as setting a routine or schedule helps us know what to expect each day. Knowing what comes next can make us feel more in control and LESS ANXIOUS. Having a close group of friends who we can rely on makes us feel secure and understood. It's the same with family traditions and having clear rules and boundaries, which give us a framework to operate within.

Finally, future plans, such as what career to pursue or what college to attend, **give us something to look forward to and work towards**. Having a plan helps reduce uncertainty about what lies ahead. I was lacking lots of these things.

At this point of my life, here's what was clear: I wanted out. I had not only stood up to the older in the gang, but I'd started working on myself too. I had made a decision and I had to follow up on it. The word **'DECISION' IN LATIN MEANS 'TO CUT OFF FROM'**, and so I committed to cutting things out of my life. Why? **Because doing so gave me more certitude that I was doing the right thing, which would get me closer to becoming my future self.** I could have died because of my dream to become someone great. If I'd got into the car with the guy called Duppy, **that could have been my last day**, but I had the belief that there was more for me out there, and so I was willing to accept whatever came my way.

SOMETIMES WE GET THINGS WRONG. I thought gangs meant belonging and safety forever, but that wasn't the case. **No one ever liked that I dreamt of things beyond the blocks.** They wanted me to be like them and commit to living and dying for a postcode or a block of flats. **Their belief was that this was the best thing for them, and because others around them held the same belief, they had the certitude that their belief was correct.**

Sometimes we have to go through things multiple times in order to fully understand if it's right for us or not. **IF YOU TRY SOMETHING NEW AND FAIL AT THE FIRST HURDLE, THEN YOU MAY HAVE QUIT TOO SOON**. What if I'd decided to stay involved in gangs because no one else left, or because getting out was too hard? **That one decision alone would have changed the entire course of my life.**

DOSAGE: Glutamate

The neurotransmitter GLUTAMATE plays a crucial role in our brain's ability to process information and form memories.

GLUTAMATE is involved in **synaptic plasticity,** which is basically the strengthening and weakening of connections in the brain, **essential for learning and memory**. When we repeat certain actions or behaviours, **GLUTAMATE** helps **strengthen the connections between cells**, making these actions more automatic over time.

THIS IS WHY REPETITION IS SO IMPORTANT.

When we engage in repetitive actions, such as studying for a test, practising a sport or following a routine, **our brain becomes more efficient at these tasks**.

The certainty we seek through repetition helps us feel more **confident and capable**.

Understanding the connection between certainty and repetition can help us make better choices. For instance, CONSISTENTLY STUDYING A LITTLE BIT EACH DAY rather than cramming the night before a test **can lead to better understanding and retention of information**. This not only boosts our grades but also **reduces stress and anxiety**.

Similarly, practising a sport regularly helps improve our skills and performance. **The more we practise, the more confident we become in our abilities.**

DO YOU THINK *RONALDO* COULD SCORE THOSE FREE KICKS IF HE HADN'T PRACTISED?

OR HOW ABOUT *STEPH CURRY?* DO YOU THINK HE COULD GET IN ALL OF THOSE THREE-POINT SHOTS WITHOUT CONSISTENT PRACTICE?

***SERENA WILLIAMS* PRACTISES UP TO SEVEN HOURS A DAY TO GET TO HER ATHLETIC STANDARD.**

***LEWIS HAMILTON* STARTED DRIVING GO-KARTS AT THE AGE OF EIGHT AND WON HIS FIRST CHAMPIONSHIP BY THE AGE OF TEN.**

If you look at the greats, they have all spent time mastering their craft — and failing in the process, but they still stuck at it.

MALCOLM GLADWELL'S popular 10,000-hour rule suggests that **mastery is achieved by investing 10,000 hours of deliberate practice**. This certainty in our skills can translate to better performance in games and competitions.

THE POWER OF ROUTINE

In our daily lives, routine and repetition help us feel more in control. Knowing that we will have dinner with our family every evening or that we will see our friends at school every day provides a sense of stability and security. **Remember, the more we engage in positive, repetitive actions, the more certain and confident we become in our abilities and our future.** *Whatever you repeat consistently, you sharpen.* When you repeat an action or a behaviour, your brain builds stronger connections and you start to lock these things in.

Repetition and routine are powerful things. When you watch athletes take part in the Olympics, they have usually put years of hard work into their training just to take part in that sport event. The fastest man ever, Usain Bolt, is regularly quoted on social media as saying he 'trained for four years to run nine seconds, and people give up when they don't see results in two months'.

When you compound consistency, things that you may not have even predicted can happen. I'M TALKING FROM EXPERIENCE. I've spoken in over 200 schools and colleges and mentored many young people, and **I've noticed that it's so easy for them to want to give up**. But the struggle, the stress, is part of the process. **Even when you're chasing something good, you're going to face obstacles – and it's healthy to see these obstacles as being there to help you**, a challenge to meet willingly. Because the really big, rewarding things in life are going to be difficult, but by repeating small, good habits within a secure and certain environment, **the little gains and improvements can become major successes**. And if your life doesn't have that security and certainty, as mine didn't, **what can you do to build towards creating that environment?**

Have you ever seen one of those videos where people find a shark or a turtle washed up on the shore? **What do they do? They help them back into the water, right? Why is that? Because that's the right environment for them.** We can't grow or flourish to become our best if we are **stuck in an**

environment that doesn't support our FUTURE-PACED SELF. Your mind is also an environment of your thoughts and ideas, so it's your responsibility to feed it with things that will help you develop more certainty. **You must be prepared to do what is right over what is easy in order to start building a secure and safe environment for yourself.**

CHAPTER 6

CONTRIBUTION - GIVE, BUT DON'T GIVE IN

I never thought I would be homeless, especially as a teenager. **I FELT LOST.** I messaged a couple of my friends to see if I could come and jam at their places that night, but it wasn't good timing. **I had to think of a plan.** I stayed sitting in the garden at the mosque, and just being there gave me a sense of peace.

There was even a moment when I was staring at the trees and plants, trying to be present, and everything that had just happened vanished from my thoughts — **the energy had shifted my focus. I knew I couldn't go back to living at home**, and me and my brother couldn't be around each other anymore. **I didn't want to tell my mum what was going on, and now people were after me.**

I waited until it got dark and made my way back to the flat, where I hopped over the garden fence, up the scaffolding and back into my room. **I already missed the smell.** I was quite proud of my room because it was something I took care of. I'd put the carpet down myself, bought and built the furniture, and **it had become my little haven**.

I grabbed a black bin bag and shoved whatever I could in there. More clothes, more books, pillows, bedsheets, the toastie machine from downstairs. I found a beat-up suitcase, which I took, filling it with some of those drinks I sold, and for a while I stood there, just staring at my room, **filled with anger, filled with sadness, asking why I had to go**.

I made my way back to the mosque, dragging the suitcase, which had no proper handle, with the black bin bag slumped over my back. I was used to carrying black bin bags from my hustling days, **but this time it wasn't a good feeling**. I got into a shop which was part of the mosque, and I prepared what was now going to be my home. I just didn't know how long for. I made space under a table, laid out some sheets, put my pillow in place and unpacked what I could without making too much of a presence. **I covered the windows with some newspaper and cloths that I found and made sure that if someone were to look in, they wouldn't know I was there.**

I couldn't fall asleep easily on the first night; my mind didn't stop racing. I went into super-deep thought mode, trying to piece everything together, trying to figure out if I could recognise the voice of the guy who had said my name through the letterbox, but I couldn't. **For the first time in a long time, I felt broken.**

There was a little window in the top left corner of the shop, which was broken, and that window let in a crazy draught. **I WAS FREEZING!** My task for the next morning was to either block the draught or find a way to bring my blanket over from my house. The window was too high up, so I couldn't fix it, **but I also really didn't want to go back. For now, no one knew I was there or where I was staying.**

I had some money left from selling those health drinks, **but that wasn't going to last a long time.** I had nowhere to cook food, and the only shops nearby were fast food, so that became my life. **I budgeted a certain amount per day, so that even if I didn't make any more money, I knew how long I could live off what I had.**

I always had a loaf of Hovis bread in the corner, a block of cheese and a bottle of ketchup. I started buying Heinz, but after a while I had to resort to buying off-brand ketchup to save that extra £1.

I was still wondering whether the guys who came looking for me were the guys from South. If it was them, then I had no idea how they'd found me, and I wanted to keep it that way.

THINGS WENT DOWNHILL FOR ME. I WAS STRUGGLING EMOTIONALLY AND MENTALLY, AND NOW MY PHYSICAL CONDITION WAS BAD. THE LACK OF TRAINING, LACK OF MOVEMENT AND LIVING OFF PROCESSED FOODS, SUGARY DRINKS AND SWEETS DIDN'T HELP. I STOPPED THINKING ABOUT DEVELOPING MY MINDSET. I HAD GIVEN UP.

How did things get this bad? I had once been the cool guy in school, the confident guy, respected, the hustler who could sell anything. **Now I lay there on the floor, homeless, shoving sweets into my mouth for comfort. I had nightmares, anxiety and low mood, and it was a huge struggle.** I remember waking up in the mornings not knowing what day it was, not really caring.

I didn't know what I was waiting for. **I had never been this miserable, but I felt unable to partake in my own rescue.** I had nothing positive to think or say about myself. **What I hated most was that I wasn't doing anything.** I was avoiding the prayer times in the mosque and I felt like I was avoiding living as a whole. **I was literally just existing.**

IT'S GOOD TO TALK

In truth, I had been through a lot of trauma. None of the guys I was around before spoke about trauma or shared how they felt.

I was still wired to think that letting out emotions meant I was weak. **It took me a long time to understand that it actually shows strength to be vulnerable.** Part of this realisation happened when one brother came to stay at the mosque for a while. **He was going through something in his personal life too.** We took comfort in each other's company — we ate together, prayed together, watched movies together — **and what I appreciated most was that we spoke.**

It felt nice to speak to a human and NOT HAVE TO LIE ABOUT WHAT WAS REALLY GOING ON. **I had been too ashamed to admit my struggles to anyone else.**

THE THOUGHTS I WAS HAVING PRIOR TO HIM COMING WERE VERY WORRYING. I CONSIDERED WHAT DIFFERENCE IT WOULD MAKE IF I WASN'T AROUND ANYMORE. I WAS IN PAIN. I WAS STRUGGLING AND I WANTED TO PUT AN END TO THOSE THINGS. AND THESE THOUGHTS RETURNED, ESPECIALLY AFTER HE LEFT TO GO BACK HOME AND I WAS ALONE AGAIN. NOW, THERE WERE ONLY THREE PEOPLE, INCLUDING THE MOSQUE'S CARETAKER, WHO KNEW I WAS THERE, AND I TRIED TO KEEP IT THAT WAY.

But there was one day when everything changed. It was a **BREAKTHROUGH MOMENT** — even if it didn't feel like one at the time. **I think I hit the lowest I could feel**, and I made the decision that as of the next day, I would start doing at least one of my daily prayers and I would find something to do, not caring if it would make me money. **I just wanted to move, to help, to add value.** I noticed that it was the first thing I had done in a while that made me feel **PROUD** – to start praying again and to have some consistency in what I was doing. **THE POWER OF ROUTINES.**

I went back to bed for a couple of hours and when I woke up this time, I didn't reach for any food or for my laptop; **I got dressed and quietly made my way into the garden**. No one had asked me to, but I started clearing the weeds, trimming bushes and doing **whatever I could to make the garden look neater**.

This time I didn't want money. **In fact, just doing the work gave me something much more valuable than the money.** I somehow became a gardener. The caretaker bought new tools that I could use and every day I would do a bit here and a bit there. Eventually there wasn't much gardening to do, **but I still wanted to be of service**, so I asked if I could shadow the carpenter who worked there daily. **I had known him for many years, and he was very softly spoken and patient with me.** I helped him build benches, repair frames, put up a huge bird cage and finally repair that broken window in the shop. When there wasn't any carpentry to do, **I still went into the workshop and would build little things for myself.**

I realised that I loved transformation. I loved gardening and now carpentry because I was taking something, using tools to improve it and watching it grow and develop step by step. I thought I was working on the garden and on the wood, **but in fact they were working on me**. It felt good to be outside and not stuck in front of my laptop, literally wasting day after day.

I had already stopped eating so much, and after a while I decided to visit my family every now and then. I would cycle there, which was about a 24-kilometre round trip, and it wasn't easy. **I started timing how long the ride took me and would challenge myself to gradually shave off seconds each time**, just like I had with my Casio watch when I ran around the block in primary school. I was achieving new **personal bests** – and, crucially, RECONNECTING with something important to my life.

I noticed a difference in the way I was feeling. **I stopped looking at what was missing and began focusing on the small differences I could make each day.** My prayers were on point, I was doing push-ups, sit-ups, cycling, I started reading my books again — **I was taking action towards change.** By this point, I was praying in the main prayer hall with whoever else came, but I made sure no one saw where I went afterwards. The only people who knew I was there were the caretaker, the security guard and my friend who had stayed there. **But one day someone else found out I was there.**

We had just finished the last prayer of the night. I got up to head into the shop, and as soon as I closed the door, someone started knocking on it. I kept quiet, in the hope that they would go away, but he persisted. He called my name, saying, 'I saw you go in — open the door!' I was scared.

But when I opened the door, I realised it was a close family friend. He asked what I was doing, how my parents were, and as he was talking to me, he noticed my bedding area and belongings. He looked me straight in the eye and asked, 'Are you living here?' He gently pushed the door open further and walked in. **I had too much respect for him to stop him. He asked me how long I had been here, and I told him it was now over six months.**

Before I could even finish explaining what happened, he said, 'Pack up your things – you're coming to mine.' I didn't want to be a bother, so I politely refused. He told me he wasn't asking. He helped me carry some things to his car. He didn't live far, but before going home he asked if I was hungry and I said very much so. He took me for a doner kebab, and it was the best doner I've ever eaten!

We got to his place and walked in through the workshop he had downstairs. I started planning where I could put my stuff down to sleep, next to his bike and some boxes, and he said, 'What are you doing? I've got a spare bedroom upstairs.'

 **I FELT LIKE THE LUCKIEST GUY IN THE WORLD!**

There was a bed, a chest of drawers, an interesting triangle-shaped wardrobe, a nice rug. **After living it rough on the shop floor, I felt like I was staying at a five-star hotel.** He told me to get settled in, and in the morning, we could talk about work and making money.

I hadn't slept on a bed in over six months. I had been sleeping under a table, the wooden top just a couple of feet away from my face — almost like a coffin. **But now I could look all the way up at a ceiling. I was so grateful.**

When we both woke up for the morning prayer, he told me I could work for him and help him out in the workshop. He would pay me daily. **I didn't care what I had to do, only that I had something to do and I would start making money again.** And this was legal work. I wondered what it would feel like to live a day without worrying if I had enough money to buy fast food or to get my clothes washed, **because that had been my reality for the past six months**.

For me, it was perfect. I was hidden away, and I had a very simple set of instructions to follow.

I had to find my rhythm with the work, but before long, I was getting it done in record time. I wasn't cutting and bagging; I was filling up bottles with cold-pressed oils and labelling them.

I felt so grateful that I had a room, a bed and a way of making a living. I had this little box made from bamboo where I kept all of my money. I would open it multiple times a day, re-count it, make sure the Queen's head was facing forward. Having money accumulating was a feeling I had missed, **and I knew this situation wasn't going to last forever, but I enjoyed it while I had it**.

That week, I reached out to some friends from my old area, my old college and the Microsoft course I'd been on, just to see who was around and if anybody wanted to meet up. **A few guys responded and we agreed to go out. I was so nervous to meet them because I'd forgotten how to act around other guys and I felt embarrassed that I was now overweight.** I feared them judging me. We sat, had a portion of chicken and chips each, and we had a great time.

None of these guys were in gangs, selling drugs or involved in anything I didn't want to be involved in either, which was very reassuring.

FOR THE WHOLE NEXT WEEK, I FELT BETTER ABOUT MYSELF.

I now had some savings, so I was able to give to charity again. This was important to me, **as giving to charity is one of the main pillars in Islam**. I was raised and taught the importance of charity, but when I was broke, there wasn't much I could give financially. **NOW I COULD GIVE BACK AGAIN**. So after Friday prayer, I would walk to the local high street and buy a bunch of toys and sweets from the pound shop. Near to where I was still living with my family friend, there was always a bunch of kids playing outside who I could tell came from families that weren't in the best financial situations. **I would hand the toys and sweets out, and I loved how happy it made the kids.**

But one day I noticed one little boy who was always the troublemaker. **This time, he stayed sitting on the swing and didn't want what I was handing out.** His English wasn't great, but I managed to work out that he was hungry. I asked the others if they were hungry and they all said yes, so I told them to wait there and jogged to the local chicken shop. **I told the owner that I was buying food for local kids and if they wanted to contribute anything free of charge then they were welcome to. And they did.** I remember ordering thirty portions of two chicken wings and chips. They gave me five bottles of fizzy drinks for free and a sleeve of plastic cups.

When the kids saw me walking back with the food and drinks, they were celebrating like it was their birthday. I saw the little boy get up from the swing and now he had the biggest smile on his face. **It lit up my day. I felt like it was one of the best things I had ever done.** What was even more beautiful was that they were calling over more kids and sharing their food with them — **none of them were greedy.** The next week I bought more food and decided that one day of pay per week would go towards this, and every Friday I would go to the chicken shop for a similar order. **I realised that in**

some way, doing something good for someone else was also a form of healing for me.

THE KINDNESS OF STRANGERS

One Friday, after I had just given out the food, one of the guys texted me saying they were out for a friend's birthday and that I should come. **I went back to my room and tried on every single piece of clothing that I owned. I felt paranoid about how I looked, as I was really out of shape. But I also knew I had to get out there again and make new friends.**

I got ready — dressed all in black with a white pair of Adidas trainers — got a fresh skin fade and was about to leave. I opened up my little bamboo box of cash and took out £100, but then paused because **I wanted to buy drinks for my friends. I took a bunch of extra notes and stashed them in my pocket.**

I got to Central London, met up with my guys and was introduced to the others. **I often hated meeting new people because I felt I wasn't good at small talk and didn't have the same kind of banter as others.** From having my stutter growing up, I became a guy of few words and still had this habit of observing people when we first met. **But I felt comfortable with these guys.** The last time I had been out with a group of this size, we were up to no good. But now we were just hanging out, enjoying each other's company.

We entered the club and I loved it. The music was loud, lasers flashing everywhere, and it took me back to when I used to dance. I was the only one not drinking alcohol, **but I didn't need it – dancing was my thing. The dance floor was my place.** Eventually I went to the bar to order another bottle of water, and when I was there a girl approached me. **It had been a long time since I'd spoken with a girl face to face, and she was beautiful.**

She seemed interested in me, asking me where I was from, what I was doing here, where I lived, what I did. **I was a little taken aback, but it felt good.** I returned the interest and offered to buy her a drink. When it was time to pay, I had to take all my money out to get to the £5 note I had in the centre of the pile, and she said, 'Woah, that's bare money. Are you rich or something?' I tried to play it cool, as if it wasn't the only money I had! I wanted to impress her. **But then a guy came up and took her away. Apparently they were together. They walked away and I saw her whispering to him.**

I made my way back to my friends instead. We were all having a good time — our hands were on each other's shoulders, we were in a circle putting our right feet in and out of the circle and shouting 'Oy oy oy', until one of the guys in my group stumbled backwards and fell over. **As he stood up, the guy who I'd seen with the girl picked him up by the throat.** I jumped in, pushed his hand off his neck and said, 'What's the issue?' The guy said, 'Your boy stepped on my fresh creps.' He told my friend to clean his shoe. **We tried to explain it was an accident, it didn't need to escalate — everyone was here to have fun.** He said calm while pointing his finger at me.

The situation made me start to feel uneasy. I knew exactly what kind of guy he was and the trouble those guys like to cause. It was time to go home. I said bye to my friends who were staying and headed out. The friends I left with lived in a different area, but I walked a couple of them to the same underground station. As we were walking, I heard someone say, 'Yo, yo, my G.' **I turned around. It was the guy from the club. I knew he wanted trouble.**

The girl who'd approached me at the bar walked over with two other guys, and the main guy said, 'Look, your friend messed up my shoes. The least you could do is buy me a new pair.' I said, 'Feel free to ask him to do that — he's back at the club, but I ain't buying you anything.' He said, 'Why not? I heard you're balling still.' **Now I clocked what had happened . . . The girl had told him about my cash.**

I turned around and walked at a fast pace, but they were following — now in front and behind me. He said, 'Fam, we can do this the easy way or the hard way. What you telling me?' **He kept one hand behind his back, which I knew meant he was**

carrying; I just didn't know what. I started raising my voice, asking him to leave me alone in the hope that some people walking by would intervene, **BUT NO ONE DID**. Then he drew his weapon. He was holding what looked like a screwdriver but with a much sharper tip, almost like an ice pick. **Either way, I didn't want to be touched with it. The other two boys I was with had run off and I felt abandoned.**

FROM MY EXPERIENCE, WHENEVER YOU MOVE TO SOMEONE, IT'S QUICK. THERE'S NO ROOM FOR CHIT-CHAT OR TIME-WASTING. I really didn't know how to get out of this. There were too many for me to fight off, this guy had a tool on me, and I could probably try to run but I wasn't in good shape. So I said, 'OK, fine, how about I pay for your shoes?' **I wished I didn't have that wad of cash on me now, but I'd made my choice.** I put my hand in my pocket and that was it — someone bottled me from behind. I could feel myself falling forward. I went down, hit my head again. They were landing their shots and then I felt two quick, cold and painful jabs to my leg.

THE GUY HAD STABBED ME TWICE IN MY RIGHT LEG.

I WAS HALF CONSCIOUS, NOT FIGHTING BACK, OUTNUMBERED AND NOT CARRYING. SOMETHING IN HIM DECIDED THAT HE STILL NEEDED TO STAB ME, AND THIS WAS THE FIRST TIME I HAD EVER BEEN STABBED. THEY TOOK MY MONEY AND RAN OFF.

A red-headed lady ran over and asked if I was OK. **She helped me sit up. I was in shock. I felt cold and my leg felt numb. I was crying and panicking.** I was scared to look at my leg. I had seen people get stabbed before, I had seen pools of blood. But as I glanced down, I was shocked. **Blood was dripping, but a lot of it was being soaked up by my jeans. I was terrified but relieved.** As crazy as it sounds, I was grateful that he had stabbed me with the screwdriver instead of a kitchen knife or blade, as that could have made things worse.

The woman stayed with me. She wanted to call an ambulance and the police to tell them I had just been robbed and stabbed. But I didn't want her to call. I was worried I would be labelled a snake and, *in truth, I didn't trust the police.* **They had wrongfully profiled me, stopped and searched me on numerous occasions, which had built a distrust of them in me.** I also knew that I wasn't getting that money back. I had to firm this loss. In hindsight, this was the wrong thing to do. **I should have had her call the ambulance and the police, but I was young and scared.**

The woman helped me to stand up, but I felt like I was going to pass out, so I told her to lie me down and, as much as I could, I propped my leg up against the shutter on the outside of a shop, which was now closed. As she lay me down, I read the graffiti on the outside of the shutter; someone had written the words 'life goes on'. **She kept insisting on calling 999 and I kept refusing.** Eventually she said she didn't want to leave me, but she really needed to get going.

This was the first time a stranger had been so nice to me, especially one who was white - I was so used to white women being scared of me or judging me, and this felt like a big deal. She taught me in that moment that strangers care, regardless of colour, regardless of race.

Before she left, she ordered me a taxi and gave me her scarf to tie up my leg, so I undid the knot and tied it securely around my quad. I could smell her perfume on the scarf and somehow the scent gave me comfort. It was like she was still there with me. **I knew I had to get up slowly so that the blood didn't rush from my head.** I started on all fours — well, all threes because I had to keep my right leg straight — but eventually got myself up and limped over to wait for my cab.

As we pulled away in the car, I opened my window to get some fresh air. **I felt that if every human was given a certain amount of patience in their life, then mine was already in the reserves.** I had silent tears running down my cheeks. **I was so angry — at myself, at the guy who stabbed me. I was angry at**

all the companies who didn't give me a job, who unknowingly could have changed the course of my life.

I stared at all the people the cab drove past, hearing all of the friends laugh, looking at the people who had their lives together, and I was jealous. Bitterly jealous. I was so fed up. I didn't want to keep living like this, always being a victim of society even when I had started over. I WAS DONE.

We got to my street, and I asked the driver how much it was. He said it had already been paid for. I told him that must be a mistake, but he said, 'No, your friend Jane called the office and paid for the trip before I picked you up.' I started crying! **Not my normal angry tears, but tears of gratitude.** I was so happy because I now knew her name — the beautiful woman who had helped me had also paid for my cab — even though I had no way of thanking her.

She had made me feel safe in a moment when I was completely vulnerable. I kept thinking that even people who I thought were my boys had turned against me: people I was in the same gang with had set me up, friends had betrayed me. But now a complete stranger had come to my rescue. **I felt seen, that she had looked at me as a human, not as a thug or thief, and it was such a good feeling.** I was focusing on this over everything else that had just happened.

I got into my room, took off my trainers and socks, undid my jeans and slowly lowered them. I kept taking deep breaths to help with my nerves, then I said, 'OK, bismillah.' (WHICH MEANS 'IN THE NAME OF GOD'.) I pulled my jeans down to my knees and looked at what had happened to my quad. **There were two holes, around 10 cm apart. I got a bowl of warm water and some towels and started cleaning myself.**

Once I had got some of the dried blood off the wounds, they stopped leaking, **and I was so happy to see that they weren't too deep**. I cleaned the wounds as much as I could, put two big plasters on them, swallowed painkillers then lay down in bed. I was so grateful to be in my bed. **I know that in situations like this, some people end up in a hospital bed and some never return home.**

I messaged a couple of my guys and asked if they got home OK. *I wanted to see if their friends who had left me had told them what happened.* I then got out my laptop, opened Facebook and started searching for Jane. I scrolled and scrolled, but I couldn't find her. I wanted to express my gratitude and explain to her how much what she did meant to me, but she was nowhere to be found.

For the next few weeks, I was obsessed with making sure my wounds didn't become infected. **I kept thinking about everything that happened that night, the money that was taken from me which I wouldn't get back.** Because the wounds weren't so serious, I was able to walk and use my legs normally quite quickly, and one of the first things I started getting back into was the gym.

I soon realised that whenever I entered the gym in a bad mood, I would always leave in a much better mood. **It was a place I could bring all my aggression and use it as fuel to better myself.** One day I also met a younger guy who wanted me to show him how to lift weights. He told me that he'd been robbed the week before, and that people made fun of him because he was marga (skinny). He said he wanted to get hench, to prove them wrong.

I understood his aggression and I wanted to help him. But I wanted him to become bigger than those guys mentally, to use the gym as a place to grow and focus on himself. Not to just look a certain way. If he held on to that anger and those tough emotions, **they would consume him**. I was talking from experience, and he knew that. He was very grateful, and we agreed to meet again the next day. **I liked that he had asked me for help.**

Before I rode off on my bike, I told him what had happened to me a few weeks back. He said that he would back me if I was going after them, but I told him that I wasn't. **I had accepted what had happened. The guy couldn't believe I was going to let them go, but I explained that these things don't end unless someone steps up.**

If someone gets robbed, they go after the person who did it, rob them and jump them. Then that person retaliates and stabs someone. The other group then goes back looking to take someone's life, **and before you know it, people are dying over what may have just been someone stepping on someone's shoe** or even being in the wrong area at the wrong time.

He looked at me and said, 'How come you know bare about these things?' I told him, 'I think differently, and in some cases I'm the only who thinks.'

THE POWER OF GIVING

It's been fourteen years since those guys took my money and stabbed my leg. And in case you're wondering, no, **I never found Jane!**

AS A YOUNG PERSON, AND EVEN AS AN ADULT, WE ARE SLAVES TO OUR EMOTIONS. MOST PEOPLE MAKE DECISIONS BASED UPON HOW THEY FEEL, AND SOMETIMES WITHOUT GIVING THINGS MUCH THOUGHT.

I've often asked myself, ***What if that guy had decided to carry a knife that day instead of a screwdriver? What if he'd stabbed me somewhere else on my body?*** Things could have been different.

I learned in my young adult years that perspective is everything. **If you change the way you look at things, the things you look at change.** In life, I believe **everything is either a lesson or a blessing.** That includes people too. It could have been a job, an experience, a holiday, a meal at a restaurant, or even just a conversation. I never tell myself it was a waste of time. **It's either something I learn from (a lesson) or something I am grateful for (a blessing).** And lessons are also blessings because they teach us mistakes that we shouldn't repeat.

So, as I look at the scars on my right leg from where the screwdriver pierced my skin, **I can see a lesson learned the hard way**. Showing off with money was obviously a mistake, but the bigger lesson was that for most of my life I had attached the importance of having money to being good enough. And that isn't a true place to derive worth from. **True worth comes from the subjects of each chapter in this book, with this, the final chapter, being about giving and contributing.**

I know that many young people aspire to be rich or become an overnight sensation as a YouTuber, influencer, streamer or through some other route. **But there is no such thing as overnight success in the way you probably think of it.** Growing up in London, you quickly realise how expensive it is, you see your parents struggle, and for many kids like me, from a young age you become income-driven. **Money is the one thing that can give your family more freedom and ease a lot of the struggle. This is why so many young people get lured into gangs with the promise of making money** – it's almost like getting hired and starting a new career without needing a CV and without facing judgement. But, as you can see, it comes at a heavy cost.

Something I have come to understand is that the secret to living is giving. For me, money and success doesn't mean much unless I am able to share them with others. And the moments that did add worth to my life, even when things were tough, were when I helped others - like when I gave to charity, when I worked at the mosque and when I gave advice in the gym.

DOSAGE: Endorphins

A type of hormone and neurotransmitter that plays a significant role in regulating mood, **ENDORPHINS** reduce stress and enhance overall wellbeing. We also release **ENDORPHINS** when we do something pleasurable. That high you can get from exercising? That's from **ENDORPHINS** being released, which also happens when we do things like meditate or listen to music that we enjoy. **I was able to feel the high from releasing ENDORPHINS through a few things I did in this chapter, too.**

Firstly, when faced with challenges and turmoil, I looked for solace in familiar environments, such as the garden at the mosque. This connection with nature triggered a sense of peace, which stimulated the release of endorphins, offering temporary relief from distress.

Human connection is another powerful catalyst for ENDORPHIN release. The companionship of my fellow brother at the mosque provided **EMOTIONAL SUPPORT and CAMARADERIE, offering a source of comfort during challenging times**. He also has a real sense of humour, and we would often be laughing throughout the day, and when we laugh our bodies also release **ENDORPHINS**.

As I gradually transitioned from a sedentary lifestyle to one filled with physical activity, such as cycling and manual labour, my body responded by releasing **ENDORPHINS. Exercise not only improves physical health but also boosts mood and reduces stress levels.** It's how I used to channel my energy and still how I start my day — an unbeatable **ENDORPHIN** release.

FINDING PURPOSE

Despite feeling lost and disconnected, I discovered a sense of purpose through acts of contribution. **Whether it was tidying up the mosque's garden or assisting the carpenter, engaging in those meaningful tasks fostered a sense of accomplishment and satisfaction.**

GIVING BACK TO THE COMMUNITY BROUGHT ME A PROFOUND SENSE OF FULFILMENT.

You may be thinking that you don't want to tidy up a garden or give to charity when you need the money yourself, **and that's OK**. But think about a time when you did help someone with something. Maybe you helped your friend with their homework, or held the door open for an elderly person. Maybe you helped your mum or dad with the housework. **Focus on that moment and think about how it made you feel. We feel good when we contribute towards others; it's a natural thing.**

As a coach, I have worked with people who have very successful businesses. They have lifestyles that most people would want, they can travel anywhere in the world and afford it, they own great cars. **But many of them in some way have often felt miserable. There's been something missing for them.** I encouraged them to start donating money to causes they cared about, but to also physically go out in to their community and **CONTRIBUTE THEIR TIME AND RESOURCES**.

I also got them to commit to making some health improvements in their lives, to put their muscles under pressure and set a target to keep themselves committed. **They couldn't believe how much better they felt and how much more meaning this added to their lives.** So you might be thinking, *Well, I don't have a business so I can't give money away.*

BUT SOMETIMES IT'S AS SIMPLE AS DOING SOMETHING NICE FOR SOMEONE ELSE WITHOUT EXPECTING ANYTHING IN RETURN.

Kindness is a subject that's very popular in a lot of schools right now, **and it's true that a little bit of kindness can have a big impact on your own life, as well as those around you**. KINDNESS is at the core of doing something nice for someone without expecting anything in return, and it's a mindset that becomes easier to adopt when you start making the choice to CONTRIBUTE. This could mean contributing to your school, home or community.

IT ONLY NEEDS TO START SMALL — JUST LIKE MY WORK DID AT THE MOSQUE — WHICH COULD MEAN HELPING OUT MORE AT HOME, OR VOLUNTEERING TO HELP WITH A PROJECT AT SCHOOL OR IN THE COMMUNITY.

But by beginning to CONTRIBUTE, building good habits around this and then making these habits become routine, as we talked about in the last chapter, **these things can compound and grow, offering you a stronger sense of purpose, self-respect and belonging**.

CONCLUSION

BREAKING THROUGH

I don't want you to have to go through tragic and traumatic life experiences just to pick up the lessons. That's why this book exists - to help you navigate your way through your teenage years successfully. At some point you might want to share this knowledge with other people you know as well.

Most of the habits adults have are formed in their teenage years, and certain belief systems are formed in the years before that. It wasn't popular for teenagers to read self-help books when I was younger. **But once I learned the power of words, the power of learning and applying new ways of thinking, my mental muscle became stronger.** You should never underestimate the power of a book. It might not even be my book, but there will be a book that you read which will completely change your perspective, and as you continue reading more books, **you begin to realise how much you didn't know**.

Growing up is hard. At times it feels like nobody understands you. Sometimes you don't even know why you feel a certain way. And the constant thoughts about what to do in the future, what job you're going to get, whether your friends are still going to be your friends, and even just getting through some of the issues you're facing at home with your family **CAN BE OVERWHELMING**. **The teenage brain often lives in fear and worries about things that haven't happened and most likely won't ever happen.**

BUT TO BE CLEAR, THERE WILL BE REAL CHALLENGES AHEAD. And that's why **RESILIENCE** is such an important quality for you to develop. Obstacles aren't in front of you to stop you long term — they may make you stop for a while, but only to reassess and then navigate your way over, under, around or through them. I mean, if you see a big red sign and it says, '1,000-volt electric fence up ahead, do not cross', I highly recommend you listen to it. **The obstacles I am talking about are**

when things feel difficult, when you experience a mental block or when other people present challenges in your life.

So many young people face difficult situations. They may move to a new school, get bullied, get into an accident or become ill; their parents might get a divorce; someone in their family might die. At some point we all go through difficult times, and just knowing that should make you realise that you are not alone.

At the end of chapter 5 I talked about the importance of developing good habits in a secure environment to deal with these obstacles, **but it is also vital to realise that you will get things wrong, make mistakes and 'fail' at some things as you go. AND THAT'S OK.** Setbacks are inevitable along the way, and indeed it's only by getting things wrong sometimes that you can learn to get it right. **So, next time you feel like you've had a setback, remember, setbacks are a set-up for a comeback!** We talked about *synaptic plasticity* back in chapter 5, and glutamate's role in building stronger connections in the brain to help us learn. **Our setbacks and mistakes help us learn just as much as our victories — in fact, more so. Behind every great breakthrough is often a series of setbacks that have been eventually overcome.**

One of the most common problems I hear young people struggling with is that they don't know what to do in the FUTURE. But, like I mentioned in the intro of this book, put your ATTENTION and INTENTION on who you want to become, your FUTURE-PACE SELF. The 'what' will figure itself out - who you are as a person is more important right now. SO DON'T STRESS, keep developing, make as many good decisions as you can, GROW YOUR RESILIENCE and have certitude in yourself.

Without knowing where you are going, you may never know when you have arrived. That's why it's so important to have an idea of who you want to become: **it's your destination.** A plane flying in the sky may hit moments of turbulence, may be slightly blown off course by the wind or may have to slow down for other reasons, but regardless, in most cases, the plane will land at its intended destination. **It's going to be the same for you.**

Throughout this book I have talked about six key themes that helped me change my path and which form part of my coaching framework, so let's recap them. **Once you understand these needs, how you meet them and that every action you take is to do with meeting a need (or more than one), it will give you a heightened level of awareness** that will help you create multiple BREAKTHROUGHS.

My initial BREAKTHROUGH was understanding this framework and realising that there was a deeper reason behind my choices. Now you can see how your choices and actions fit into these six themes.

FOUNDATIONS
(AND HOW TO BUILD ON THEM)

Humans need to develop and to know we are progressing. If we don't feel like we are growing, then we don't feel like we are doing anything with our lives.

CONNECTION
(AND HOW TO RESIST PEER PRESSURE)

Humans need to experience a healthy version of love and a sense of belonging. It helps us function and provides a sense of connection to something beyond ourselves.

RESPECT
(WITH AN EMPHASIS ON SELF-RESPECT)

Humans like to feel that we matter, that we make a difference and that in our own way we are unique.

THE RUSH
(WHY THE RIGHT KIND OF UNCERTAINTY AND ADRENALINE RELEASE IS SO IMPORTANT)

Humans need a change in routine. We need new stimuli and things to excite us.

SECURITY
(WHY REAL FREEDOM AND SUCCESS STARTS WITH CERTAINTY AND FEELING SAFE)

Humans need to feel safe and secure with both our choices and surroundings.

CONTRIBUTION
(WHY DOING, GIVING AND KINDNESS ARE THE KEYS TO SUCCESS)

Humans need to contribute to something greater than themselves while positively contributing to the future version of themselves.

These six elements, in harmony and in balance, have been the keys to me changing my life, and I hope they can help you improve yours.

It may be that you need more work on some than others, or that you're better stocked in one department than another, but you can work on improving that. Think about the activities you can do every day to fulfil these areas — **so you can develop, connect, feel special, add variety, find certainty and contribute**. You can also better understand more about life and other people. **You can look at a person or situation and make a note of which needs they're meeting**, and then you can understand their behaviour.

This allows you to be a more supportive friend and family member to the people around you.

Understanding these key themes now has allowed me to see that, strangely, being in a gang actually helped me meet a lot of these needs:

JOINING AND WORKING MY WAY UP IN THE GANG — FOUNDATIONS AND HOW TO BUILD ON THEM

BEING ACCEPTED AND BUILDING A BOND WITH THE GANG MEMBERS — CONNECTION

MAKING A NAME FOR MYSELF AND GAINING RESPECT — RESPECT AND SIGNIFICANCE

TAKING PART IN THE DAY-TO-DAY NEFARIOUS ACTIVITIES — UNCERTAINTY AND VARIETY

HAVING PROTECTION AND A WAY TO MAKE MONEY — SECURITY AND ROUTINE

BEING PART OF A MUCH BIGGER ORGANISATION — CONTRIBUTION

For many people, gang life is their identity. It is their family. Forget me; **if another young person didn't have a family or support network, had no work opportunities and grew up in an area with crime and violence, would it be difficult to understand why this is a natural progression for them?** On top of social exclusion and so many other unfortunate realities, when I break it down, these individuals are just meeting their needs and modelling what they have been exposed to. **They are listening to their human needs. The only problem is that they have limited knowledge of how to meet those needs in more positive ways.** THEY'RE JUST TRYING TO SURVIVE, exactly like I did for so many years. But that's not life. **We should be living to thrive, not to survive within a system or mindset that keeps us limited.**

I've been contacted by seven prisons to deliver mindset and reform coaching. I've also been into juvenile prisons to coach and speak to the young offenders, **and there's nothing that makes me sadder than to see all those young people in there who got caught up in a lifestyle**. Of course, actions have repercussions, and some of them do deserve to be in there for the choices they made, but it's made me ask myself, *What if more young people knew what I knew? What if they understood what I have been figuring out for years? What if they had better role models to show them there is another way?*

My intention with this book from the start was to keep things 100. **I want to be real with you all**, and to do that I've shared a lot of my history — **some of which I'm not very proud of now, even if I've definitely learned from it**. But one of the clearest things I remember about being a young boy was that at each age I always wanted to be older so that I could do more cool things. But let me tell you something: ENJOY YOUR YOUTH. These are the years to have fun, to be happy and fulfilled.

Sometimes kids think that when they are an adult, no one will tell them what to do, and they won't have to go to school or have any problems. **This couldn't be more wrong.** Sure, our responsibilities change, but here's something that many adults say:

'I wish I could be younger again.' **So if you're able to, try to enjoy the ride.**

I don't know what area or city you live in or what your life situation is like right now, but here's what I do know: **at some point you're going to be in a situation where you have to make a tough decision.** That decision could be to move schools, to change clubs, to end a friendship and block them. It could be to inform someone because your friend is in trouble or making really bad life choices. It might even be to get away from your own relatives.

Sometimes it's hard to do the right thing, but at the end of the day, the right thing is always the right thing to do. And if it's to do with keeping you or someone else safe, then you shouldn't hesitate.

No one is perfect; we are all doing the best we can with the best we've got. But whatever is bothering you or challenging you now, it will pass. What you can do is BELIEVE IN YOURSELF and make a commitment to becoming a better version of yourself, to set yourself new personal bests **and then help others to do the same**. In simple terms, you need to know who you want to be, remove any doubt and have values that you live by.

The ultimate key to unlocking anything is belief backed by enduring faith. **Whatever you decide to believe, you have made a reality for yourself. SO MAKE SURE YOU DEVELOP BELIEFS THAT ENCOURAGE YOU, EMPOWER YOU AND ELEVATE YOU**, not ones that say you're not good enough or can't do it.

And that's not to say it will come easily. Being a man of faith, and being a man who has lost his faith at times, **my beliefs have been tested**. But if you truly want to experience a better life and achieve success, **then you must go through the process before getting to the promise**. I never had the framework I have given you in this book when I was a teenager, **but you now have in your hands a powerful tool. One that I believe is a BREAKTHROUGH in itself.**

Be better than you were yesterday and build a future in your mind that compels you, because once you can see it in your mind and believe it with your heart, you will feel it in your hands — you are only one breakthrough away from success.

Omar

RESOURCES

CRIME/LEGAL SUPPORT

ABIANDA *abianda.com*
A London-based social enterprise working with young women affected by gangs and county lines.

THE BEN KINSELLA TRUST *benkinsella.org.uk*
One of the leading anti-knife crime charities in the UK, set up following the tragic murder of Ben Kinsella in 2008.

FAMILIES OUTSIDE *familiesoutside.org.uk*
Supports families in Scotland affected by imprisonment.

FEARLESS *fearless.org*
A service that allows individuals to pass on information about crime 100% anonymously.

HOWARD LEAGUE FOR PENAL REFORM
howardleague.org
An organisation working for less crime, safer communities and fewer people in prison. They run a confidential legal service for young people under twenty-one, including those in prison.

JUST FOR KIDS LAW *justforkidslaw.org*
Works with and for young people to ensure their legal rights are respected and promoted, and that their voices are heard and valued.

LIVES NOT KNIVES *livesnotknives.org*
A youth-led charity that works to prevent knife crime, serious youth violence and school exclusions by engaging, educating and empowering.

NATIONAL CRIMINAL JUSTICE ARTS ALLIANCE *artsincriminaljustice.org.uk*
Their vision is to ensure the arts are used within the criminal justice system as a springboard for positive change.

NIACRO *niacro.co.uk*
Supports children, young people and families who are affected by imprisonment, who have offended or who are perceived to be vulnerable to offending.

PRISON ADVICE AND CARE TRUST (PACT) *prisonadvice.org.uk*
Provides support for prisoners, people with convictions and their families.

POWER THE FIGHT *powerthefight.org.uk*
A charity that tackles violence affecting young people by creating long-term solutions for sustainable change.

SAFE4ME *safe4me.co.uk*
Provides educators, service providers and parents with information and resources to help educate, guide and support children and young people to keep safe.

SPURGEONS *spurgeons.org*
Provides support to help improve the lives of children and their families who are affected by a parent being in prison.

STEEL WARRIORS *steelwarriors.co.uk*
An anti-knife crime charity that melts down knives taken off the streets and recycles the steel into outdoor street gyms.

UNLOCK *unlock.org.uk*
Provides a voice and support for people who are facing stigma and obstacles because of their criminal record.

USER VOICE *uservoice.org*
Created for and by people who have been in prison and on probation, giving a voice to the most marginalised people.

THE MIX *themix.org.uk*
The Mix has information and support for anyone between the ages of thirteen and twenty-five. Connect with experts and peers who provide support and tools for everything from homelessness to finding a job, from money to mental health, and from break-ups to drugs.

BLUEPRINT FOR ALL *blueprintforall.org*
Formerly the Stephen Lawrence Charitable Trust, they work with young people, communities and organisations to create an inclusive society in which everyone, regardless of race, ethnicity or background, is provided with tangible opportunities to thrive.

RUNAWAY HELPLINE *runawayhelpline.org.uk*
Run by the UK charity Missing People and has been supporting young people for many years. Staff and volunteers are trained professionals who want to help young people through anything they are finding tough.

MENTAL HEALTH SUPPORT

SAMARITANS *samaritans.org*
Offers listening and support services over the phone or on email to people in need of help.

CHILDLINE *childline.org.uk/get-support*
Offers a free, confidential service for young people to talk to counsellors via phone, online chat or email.

HUB OF HOPE *hubofhope.co.uk*
A database of local and national mental health support and services.

MIND *mind.org.uk*
Provides mental health advice and support, and campaigns to raise awareness and improve services.

CALM *thecalmzone.net*
Runs campaigns to raise awareness and challenge the stigma that stops people talking about suicide and asking for help.

HEADS TOGETHER *headstogether.org.uk*
Works to challenge the stigma around mental health and to help people open up and ask for help.

MENTAL HEALTH MATES *mentalhealthmates.co.uk*
A network of peer support groups run by people who are experiencing their own mental health issues. They meet regularly to walk, talk and share their experiences without judgement.

YOUNG MINDS *youngminds.org.uk*
The UK's leading charity fighting for children and young people's mental health.

OUR TIME *ourtime.org.uk*
Provides information and workshops for children and young people whose parents or carers are experiencing mental health problems.

CRISIS TEXT LINE *www.crisistextline.org*
A service that offers free, 24/7 mental health support via text message.

MENTAL HEALTH SUPPORT- AUSTRALIA

HEADSPACE *headspace.org.au*
Offers mental and physical health support services to young people across Australia.

KIDS HELPLINE *kidshelpline.com.au*
A free, confidential 24/7 online and phone counselling service for young people aged five to twenty-five in Australia.

LIFELINE SOUTH AFRICA *lifelinesa.co.za*
Offers a 24-hour phone counselling service to anyone in South Africa who is struggling, and aims to improve emotional wellness for individuals and communities.

SOUTH AFRICAN FEDERATION FOR MENTAL HEALTH *www.safmh.org*
National organisation that works with the community to help provide high-quality mental health care.

YOUTHLINE *youthline.co.nz*
Provides support to young people aged twelve to twenty-four in New Zealand, including a 24/7 helpline (via phone, email, text and webchat) as well as free face-to-face counselling, mentoring, and school and community programmes.

0800 WHAT'S UP? *whatsup.co.nz*
A free counselling helpline and webchat service for children and teenagers in New Zealand, run by Barnados New Zealand.

MENTAL HEALTH SUPPORT - *INDIA*

THE MINDS FOUNDATION *mindsfoundation.org*
An organisation based in India which works to remove the stigma around mental health illnesses and improve access to care.

MANAS FOUNDATION *manas.org.in*
A New Delhi-based organisation that promotes psychological health and wellbeing and offers sessions with psychologists.

POSITIVE MASCULINITY

WHITE RIBBON UK *whiteribbon.org.uk*
Charity working to get men and boys involved in ending violence against women and girls, by building communities, holding policymakers accountable, campaigning for greater awareness and educating young people.

BEYOND EQUALITY *beyondequality.org*
Works with young boys and men to help them engage with creating safer communities, preventing gender-based violence and creating gender equality.

GOOD MEN PROJECT *goodmenproject.com*
Online hub sharing information and helping people participate in the conversations around masculinity and the way men's roles are changing in modern life.

ACKNOWLEDGEMENTS

My deepest gratitude goes to my incredible children, Yusuf and Yaseen, whose existence inspires me to be a better man, and to my wife, Karolina, whose unwavering support and belief in me make everything possible. To my family and friends, thank you for your love, strength, and encouragement throughout this journey. A special thank you to the amazing team at Hachette for believing in the power of this story and helping bring it to life. And to everyone who has been a part of my journey — whether in ways big or small — your impact has been felt, and I am truly grateful.